OUT
OF
THE
DEPTHS

ALSO BY ANTON T. BOISEN

THE EXPLORATION OF THE INNER WORLD
A Study of Mental Disorder and Religious Experience

RELIGION IN CRISIS AND CUSTOM
A Sociological and Psychological Study

PROBLEMS IN RELIGION AND LIFE
*A Manual for Pastors, with Outlines for the Study of Personal
Experience in Social Situations*

HYMNS OF HOPE AND COURAGE
A Service-Book for Use in Hospitals

OUT
OF
THE
DEPTHS

AN AUTOBIOGRAPHICAL
STUDY OF
MENTAL DISORDER AND
RELIGIOUS EXPERIENCE

Anton T. Boisen

HARPER & BROTHERS, PUBLISHERS, NEW YORK

TO THE MEMORY
OF
WILLIAM LOWE BRYAN
MY TEACHER
AND FRIEND

CONTENTS

FOREWORD

THIS IS MY OWN CASE RECORD. I offer it as a case of valid religious experience which was at the same time madness of the most profound and unmistakable variety. In this record I have brought together such material as may throw light upon the origin, meaning, and outcome of that experience. This I have done not from any love of dwelling upon matters which are often painful and delicately personal, and certainly not from any desire to display them to others. I have written it because now for forty years I have been making it my business to inquire into the problems here involved, and my own case is the one I know best. It may indeed constitute a biasing factor which needs to be discounted, but it affords also the firsthand evidence which is the basis of any authority I may claim as an explorer in this field. It gives support to my central thesis that certain forms of mental disorder and certain forms of religious experience are closely interrelated. Mental disorder is, I hold, the price humanity has to pay for having the power of choice and the capacity for growth, and in some of its forms it is a manifestation of healing power analogous to fever or inflammation in the body.

That this record centers in a love story is explained by the fact that I could not offer an adequate interpretation of the experiences under consideration without taking into account the part played by the beloved friend to whose memory my *Exploration of the Inner World* is dedicated. In many ways that

9

story is a tragedy. She died too soon and we cannot have the benefit of the light she might have thrown upon this record. But she did agree that this story, which is hers as well as mine, should be shared with others. I offer it with the deepening conviction that it gives evidence of the guiding hand of an Intelligence beyond our own.

ANTON T. BOISEN

Elgin, Illinois
July 1, 1960

ACKNOWLEDGMENTS

First of all and above all, this book owes its existence to Fred Eastman, sometime professor in the Chicago Theological Seminary, who not only preserved the documents upon which it is based but also helped to preserve the author himself and enable him to pull through the trying experience with which it deals.

The writer is also deeply indebted to the Rt. Rev. Norman B. Nash, who was the first to open the door into the new field of work with which this book deals and who through the years has been a stanch supporter of the movement for the clinical training of students for the ministry.

Both these men have read the manuscript, offering valuable suggestions, and they have helped to overcome the hesitation which the author has felt regarding its publication.

To the Chicago Theological Seminary and to its former president, Arthur Cushman McGiffert, Jr., I am indebted for their support over many years of an undertaking about which at first they had many misgivings; also to the Elgin State Hospital for opening its doors to me and to my students. My indebtedness extends to unnumbered others, among whom I think especially of Francis McPeek and Mrs. Marjorie Peters Bower, both of whom have had an important part in the making of this book.

In the decision to publish it, I have been guided by the hope that it may help to throw light upon the profounder struggles of the human soul, and lead the way toward further exploration.

A. T. B.

OUT
OF
THE
DEPTHS

I

ANCESTRY AND
SOCIAL BACKGROUND

SO FAR AS I CAN DISCOVER, our family record is relatively free from abnormalities such as those with which this study deals. Nonetheless, the social background is important in any attempt to understand a person. I shall therefore begin with a brief consideration of my ancestors and their social setting.

Concerning the family of my father, Hermann B. Boisen, I know only a little. His father, Johannes F. O. Boisen, belonged to a German-speaking family in the province of Schleswig. His father's father was an organist and music teacher. In the difficulties between Schleswig-Holstein and Denmark in the 1860's, Grandfather Boisen favored German intervention. He was apparently a man of standing and influence. Following German occupation, he was appointed Amtsrichter in the Island of Alsen. Before that time the family lived in Flensburg. About the time my father was approaching the completion of his work for the doctorate at the University of Wuerzburg his father met with serious financial reverses. He died when past seventy. He was a tall, heavy-set man, some six feet four inches in height and weighing about two hundred and fifty pounds.

My father's mother, Marie Andersen Boisen, also belonged to a German-speaking family in Schleswig. She was the daughter of a Lutheran pastor. My father always spoke of her with the greatest respect and tenderness as a wise and devoted mother and a capable manager. She lived to be past eighty. Besides my father there were four other children who lived to maturity. Three of these died of tuberculosis. This was probably owing to the fact that they had lived in an old stone castle on the Island of Alsen, a building with massive, damp walls. The only surviving members of the family are now living in the city of Oldenburg, having been compelled to leave Schleswig after that province reverted to Denmark. I have never seen any of my German relatives, but we keep in touch with each other by correspondence.

My father came to this country in April, 1869. Unable to complete his doctorate because of his father's financial situation, he felt that there would be less red tape to contend with in the New World. He went first to the home of some relatives in St. Paul. From there he went to Belleville, Indiana. There his genius as a teacher attracted instant attention, and in the late fall of 1870, on the recommendation of some members of the De Pauw University faculty and after a visit by Professor Richard Owen, he was appointed to fill a vacancy in the chair of modern languages at Indiana University.

The maternal ancestors of my mother, Louise Wylie Boisen, came from England in the seventeenth century and settled in New Jersey. Her great-grandfather, John Dennis, was a wealthy New Brunswick merchant who, during the War of the Revolution, served as treasurer of the province of New Jersey. His son, Richard, her grandfather and my great-grandfather, was a Philadelphia merchant who made and lost three considerable fortunes. During the War of 1812 he commanded the Sixteenth Infantry. Richard Dennis was married three times. His third marriage was to Susanna Salter Smith, whom he met when they were both having their portraits painted by Rembrandt Peale. She was fifteen at the time, he thirty-six. His father disapproved but wrote expressing the hope that "the new spouse might prove a durable blessing." Eleven children were born to this marriage, eight of whom lived to the age of seventy-five or more. My grandmother, Rebecca Dennis Wylie, was one of these. She was born in Germantown just across the street from the old Chew House, which we used to see pictured in our American history books.

My mother's paternal grandfather, my great-grandfather, was Samuel Brown Wylie, who came to Philadelphia in 1797 from the North of Ireland, where, as a young man, he had been involved in political difficulties. In 1803 he became pastor of the newly organized Reformed Presbyterian Church of Philadelphia. This pastorate he held until his death in 1852. In addition to serving as pastor of this church, which became a large and influential one, he conducted a classical school for boys. He also conducted a theological school for the Reformed Presbyterian Church. In 1828 he became professor of Latin and Greek and the Oriental languages at the University of Pennsylvania. That position he held for twenty years. During the last ten years he was vice-provost of the University. He is described as a vigorous man and a prodigious worker. According to family tradition he was accustomed to take only four hours sleep out of the twenty-four, getting up at two or three o'clock in the morning in order to study undisturbed. He ruled his household with a rod of iron. By that I do not mean that he was harsh or stern. His writings[1] and letters show him to have been affectionate and

[1] Cf. his *Life of Alexander McLeod* (New York: Charles Scribner's Sons, 1855).

gifted in the expression of his feelings. He was both loved and feared, and he struck awe into the hearts of his sons and of other boys as well. He had a reputation for understanding boys and knowing how to deal with difficult cases.

His wife, Margaret Watson Wylie, my great-grandmother, was a gentle, devoted woman. She came from Pittsburgh, where her father owned a farm which is now in the heart of that city. This Pittsburgh property made her husband's household economically secure. She lived to the good old age of ninety.

There were five children in her household: Theophilus, my grandfather, who was born in 1810; Theodorus, some years younger, who in 1843 became co-pastor of his father's church and continued as pastor until his death in 1898; and three daughters. Two of the daughters married Reformed Presbyterian clergymen. The other daughter, Elizabeth Louise, who died at the age of sixteen, was a close friend of my grandmother, Rebecca Dennis. It was through her that she and my grandfather met and for her that my mother was named.

As a boy, Theophilus Wylie attended his father's classical school. He is said to have read two books of Caesar by the time he was eight years old. Certainly he was almost as much at home in Latin as in English. He was also an able Greek scholar. His college work was done at the University of Pennsylvania. His major interests were in the sciences. He was also interested in painting and had dreams of becoming an artist. His father, however, wanted him to study for the ministry. As a dutiful son he yielded to his father's wishes. It was a great relief to him when his father finally decided in favor of his becoming a teacher. In 1837 he went out to the wilds of Indiana to join the faculty of the state university in Bloomington, of which Andrew Wylie, a nephew of his father, was president. He had been given the choice of the chair of "pure mathematics" or that of "mixed mathematics." He had chosen the former and had spent several months brushing up on his algebra and geometry and calculus, when word came that he had been appointed to the chair of mixed mathematics. This, being interpreted, meant physics, chemistry, geology, and natural history. He stayed on at Indiana until his retirement in 1886. With the exception of a period of two and a half years during which he taught at Miami University in Oxford, Ohio (1852-54), he was thus in continuous active service at Indiana University for forty-six and a half years. His special field was natural philosophy, but at one time or another he taught almost every course in the curriculum except moral philosophy. He was a really good teacher and a thorough scholar. In addition to his teaching he served for many years as librarian of the University, and for thirty years he was pastor of the New Side Reformed Presbyterian Church, one of the four psalm-singing Presbyterian churches in Bloomington during the middle of the nineteenth century.

In 1838, after the year's probation upon which he had insisted, Theophilus Wylie returned to Philadelphia to marry Rebecca Dennis and take her back with him to Bloomington. It required two weeks to make the trip. They traveled part way by rail, part way by stagecoach, part way by canal boat to Pittsburgh, then by boat down the Ohio to Louisville, and thence by stage to Bloomington. My mother, born in Bloomington in 1839, was their oldest child. My grandfather wanted to name her "Erasmia" after his favorite philosopher, but my grandmother rebelled. They agreed on "Louise." There were five other children who lived to maturity, one sister and four brothers. One of the brothers lost his life in the Civil War. Another died of tuberculosis.

In 1859 my grandfather bought the large brick house on East Second Street, in Bloomington, built in 1833 by his cousin, President Andrew Wylie. Here the family lived until my grandmother's death in 1913 at the age of one hundred and one years. This house is now owned by the University and plans are under way to restore it.

My mother, who died in 1930 at the age of ninety-one, got her schooling in Bloomington at the "Female Seminary" which was conducted by Mrs. E. J. McFerson,[2] a sister of Professor Daniel Read of the University. In 1852, when the family moved to Oxford, Ohio, she enrolled in Professor Scott's school for girls. About the same time Mrs. McFerson moved her Female Seminary to Glendale, Ohio. My mother joined her there as a student and later taught in that school. It may be of interest to note that at Oxford her music teacher was Dr. Scott's daughter, Carrie, who married Benjamin Harrison, and that at Glendale her bosom friend was Mrs. McFerson's daughter, Parke, who married John W. Foster, the man who in later years became Harrison's secretary of state. My mother was one of the first women to enroll at Indiana University. After her graduation in 1871 she taught at the University of Missouri, of which Daniel Read was at that time president. She left at the end of her first year to be married to her teacher of modern languages at Indiana University. I entered the world in 1876 as their first child.

[2] J. A. Woodburn, *History of Indiana University, 1820-1902* (Bloomington: Indiana University Press, 1940), p. 131.

II

EARLY YEARS

MY EARLIEST RECOLLECTIONS date from about the age of two and a half years. I can recall somewhat hazily a piece of bread and butter and sugar, a red dress, and a stove. I was inside the dress, attempting to get outside of the bread and butter, and I sat down on the hearth of the stove. The dress caught fire and the scene was burned into my memory. This happened in the Maxwell house at the corner of College Avenue and Fourth Street in Bloomington, Indiana. This house, as I recall it, was an L-shaped building two stories high on the Fourth Street side, which we occupied. On the College Avenue side was the one-story office of old Dr. James Darwin Maxwell, son of Dr. David H. Maxwell, who is generally recognized as the founder of Indiana University. At this time Bloomington was a town of perhaps twenty-five hundred. Its sidewalks consisted chiefly of flagstones and its streets were mostly of red clay, macadamized here and there with broken limestone. The University, where my father and my grandfather taught, occupied at that time a ten-acre tract at the south end of College Avenue two blocks from the Maxwell house.

From about the same period comes another memory, this time of Dr. Maxwell's office. I went in with my father and we waited until a big man came in and took a seat. Young Dr. James D. Maxwell did something to him. Then he did something to me that hurt. I learned later that I had been vaccinated and that the big man was Professor David Starr Jordan, a friend of my father's, and that, according to the approved procedure of those days, the doctor got from him the serum which he rubbed into my arm.

I can recall also a cane, a black cane with a white handle, of which I was very proud, and a visit to my grandparents in the big house on Second Street. Some cousins from Dakota were visiting there and five-year-old Dick, the youngest, who was two years my senior, was much interested in my cane. He offered to show me a trick with it. Immediately I consented. He then took the cane, placed it between two sticks of wood and brought an ax down upon it, explaining that canes were "dude stuff" and that they were not tolerated among he-men.

My sister, Marie, now Mrs. Morton Clark Bradley, was born in 1879, when I was two years and eleven months old, while we were living on North Walnut Street between Seventh and Eighth Streets. My memories of that event center around the fact that I was taken to a neighbor's, the Fees, and that I was not permitted to go home. However, I was given some fresh-baked gingersnaps, and I was well content.

My earliest memories of my mother are of her singing. She had had excellent training in music, having studied, among others, with Mme Rivé of Cincinnati. She was a good pianist and had a sweet contralto voice, singing either soprano or alto. Music was an important part of my father's plan of education, and he was particularly fond of some of the fine old German hymns and folk songs. He was not a singer himself, but he loved having my mother sing them for us. She was very fond of

Stephen Foster, but his songs did not make much of an impression upon me in the early years. Mother was gentle and retiring. Throughout her dealings with me she relied on persuasion rather than compulsion. She made me feel bad when I did not do as I ought to do.

My father was the dominant member of the household. He was always full of life and full of ideas, interested in everything that went on. His was a contagious enthusiasm which carried others along with him. He was a great lover of nature, of trees and shrubs and flowers, and he took great interest in teaching me the names of the trees. It was he who did the landscaping at the old home, and in addition to modern languages he also taught botany at the University.

I remember him as a tall man with a full beard who took time to do things for me and with me. On occasion he would punish. He could be stern but he was always kind. On two occasions which I can recall, the offense was lying. I do not remember what it was about, but I do remember his explaining very carefully why I was being punished and how many blows I was to receive. He always set a maximum and a minimum, the minimum being employed if I refrained from crying. He was always careful to make it clear that there was no change in his love for me and that the punishment was not arbitrary but a necessary consequence of what I had done.

There came a time not long after my sister's birth when I missed my father. I learned later that he had resigned in the middle of the school year of 1879-80 because of the dismissal of a colleague. He felt that serious injustice had been done. He therefore submitted his resignation and left the University, with nothing in view but selling books.

It seems that on other occasions he acted impulsively. Once

when a group of students had disappointed him in some signal way, he was seized with despair, felt that he had failed as a teacher, and got on a train and left town. After several days he returned quietly and took his place in the classroom.

On another occasion the professor of English made a brilliant speech before some university gathering. Unfortunately it followed almost word for word a speech by some other man, which my father had happened to read. My father was not one who could tolerate dishonesty and he blurted out his discovery in faculty meeting. He thus brought a good deal of trouble upon himself as well as upon the offending colleague.

After several discouraging months my father was fortunate enough to be appointed to a vacancy in Williams College in Massachusetts with the understanding that if he made good, the appointment would be permanent. Therefore we moved to Williamstown. There he continued to spend a good deal of his leisure time teaching me to distinguish the different kinds of trees by means of leaves and bark. He also took us out frequently to enjoy the mountain scenery.

Shortly after I had passed my fourth birthday, while we were living in Williamstown, I had the experience of being circumcized. Quite spontaneously, it seemed, there had developed a sex-organ excitation which seemed beyond the normal. I can recall my parents' anxious concern and the consultation with the doctor. He was sure it was due to local irritation, and the operation was performed. As a matter of fact, the trouble lay in a more than average interest in matters eliminative and sexual. I may add that I do not remember ever overhearing or seeing anything in the behavior either of adults or of other children which might explain it. Since it was thus primarily psychical, the treatment failed to correct it. The following summer, while at the home of my grandparents in Bloomington, this interest led to some mutual explorations with a boy cousin about a year younger. We were promptly caught and my mouth was washed out with soap and water. This treatment seems to have put an end to the trend for the time being. The horror on my mother's face and her volunteered promise that she would not tell my father are impressions which still remain.

With the end of that year there came a bitter disappointment. There was a change of administration at Williams College. My father's appointment was not made permanent and we had to return to Bloomington. That he had made good seems abundantly clear. One of his students at Williams, Starr Willard Cutting, subsequently head of the German Department at the University of Chicago, told me years later that he considered my father one of the most gifted teachers he had ever known and David Starr Jordan had recommended him "without hesitation" as the most effective teacher of languages he had ever known. But the new president wanted a faculty of Ph.D.'s, and my father did not have that degree.

Following the disappointment at Williams, my father taught for two years in the public schools of Boston. There he prepared two textbooks, his *First Course in German* and his *German Prose*. He also did outstanding work as a teacher, attracting the attention of such educators as Colonel Francis Parker and William T. Harris, the U.S. Commissioner of Education. By the end of the first year he was able to bring us to Martha's Vineyard, where he taught in the Summer Institute. In the fall of 1882 we moved to Cambridge. There we lived on Broadway, near Inman Street, not far from Harvard University. I was at that time six years of age, and I had the benefit of some good kindergarten instruction.

The next year, 1883, my father received a call from the newly organized Lawrenceville School near Princeton, New Jersey. We were all very happy over this. It brought us near my mother's ancestral home in Philadelphia, where her uncle, my grandfather's brother Theodorus, was a leading pastor; and the salary of $3,600 a year was, for those days, relatively high. My father felt that he had found just the right opening.

According to the plan of the school each master had his own family of boys. They all lived together under one roof, beginning each morning with prayers, eating together in the common dining room, and closing the day with prayers. My father rejoiced in the many opportunities thus afforded to get acquainted with his boys in Davis House, which had been assigned to us.

At Lawrenceville he continued his efforts to help me become acquainted with the trees. He also took me frequently to the gymnasium and sought to teach me to perform certain simple exercises.

I recall in particular one occasion when I went with him and several of the boys on a hike. We were to search for trailing arbutus, which was reported as growing nearby. This was his favorite flower, and he promised me a silver dollar for the first leaf I found. It was a long hike, some ten or twelve miles as I recall it. I came through without the dollar, but with enough energy left to demand inclusion in a drive he was making to Trenton. When he refused, I set up a loud wail. His response was to put me in a dress and give me a doll to play with. This he did somewhat playfully, saying that boys of seven who could go on long hikes were too big to cry. My recollection is that I at once stopped crying and the dress was promptly removed. I caught his spirit, and felt that he was perhaps proud of the fact that I had gone through with the hike.

My father always worked under tension, very high tension,

and he had both the strengths and the weaknesses which go with such a temperament. In any case, at the age of thirty-eight he burned himself out, dying of heart failure on January 16, 1884.

There had been two previous attacks, one the year before, another several weeks before; but apparently the gravity of the situation was not recognized. The end came about seven o'clock in the evening just after my sister and I had gone to bed. All was over in a few minutes. I can remember the excitement, then the quiet, and my mother's gentle sobbing. She took it bravely; but she did little with her music afterward.

My father thus died when I was only three months past my seventh birthday, but his memory, reinforced by my mother's picture of him and that of others who knew him, has remained a potent force in my life, one which for me has been associated with my idea of God.

Memorial services were held for him in Lawrenceville and in Bloomington. At Indiana University the address was given by David Starr Jordan.[1] This address has been of particular importance to me. I give it in full:

"Think of me always at my best, Davy" was the last request of Steerforth to David Copperfield. And to-day, as we meet to do honor to the memory of Professor Boisen, it behooves us to cast aside all other recollections and to think of him only at his best, for men of genius have ever their ebb and flow. All such memories we shall lay aside forever. For at his best what a man he was! So broad, so fine, so tender, so intense. A teacher who inspired all with whom he came in contact; who touched everything with life and made even the vagaries of the German article a thing of beauty and of light. A linguist to whom all languages and all literatures came as a natural inheritance, who rejoiced alike in the misty dreams of the stormy Northmen, the homely life of the Plattdeutscher, and the polished

---

[1] *Indiana Student,* February, 1884 (cf. Woodburn, *op. cit.,* pp. 355-58).

imagery of the Greeks; a lover of nature whose knowledge of trees and plants and flowers was the envy of professional botanists; one who saw everything in nature and had a heart open to all sweet influences of flower and bird and sky; a man of boundless energy who threw into the most trifling duty the full strength of his mighty soul. Thus sometimes his work seemed like that of a mighty engine fastened to a common cart, for he never did all that he could have done either as a teacher or a writer. The time had not yet come when the world could put him to its highest use.

My pleasantest memories of Professor Boisen are associated with his love of nature and his fine appreciation of German literature, German life, German history and German scenery. He could speak of each of these in a strain of vigor and of poetry such as one rarely hears. He once laid out a tramp for us through Holstein and Thuringia and was never weary of telling us of the beautiful things we should see on the road, the rocks and lakes and glens and castles, the Inselberg, the Liebenstein, and the forest-hidden Ukleisee, which, alas, we shall never see with his eyes.

When I first visited this city five years ago, Professor Boisen, as the highest courtesy he could show me, took me out in his carriage to see the treasure of Bloomington. It is a steep hill-side, covered with trees and carpeted with a flower seldom seen in the west, the trailing arbutus, the may-flower of our Pilgrim fathers.

I never had a more delightful companion. Never was I with one who saw more or better. Every bush was to him an old friend. Every leaf he knew. Every bud was to him the promise of an opening flower and to see a flower in the early spring a thing worth living for.

To me the woods and glens around Bloomington are full of memories of him and with the arbutus-covered hill-side his name should be forever associated.

IN THE OLD HOME

Following my father's death we returned to Grandfather Wylie's home in Indiana. For my grandparents this was the beginning of a very trying period. In 1885, the year following our return, there came a change of administration in the University. David Starr Jordan took over. At that time thirty-four years of age, he had already won world-wide recognition as an authority on fishes and he was soon to be recognized as one of America's really great university presidents. He wanted a faculty of young specialists and a university in which the student would have a chance to participate in actual research while still an undergraduate.[2] This meant change, and my grandfather was the outstanding representative of the old order that had to go. His desire to round out fifty years of service was therefore not honored and he was retired at the end of his forty-ninth year of teaching.

To make the situation worse, Uncle Brown Wylie, his son, my mother's brother, who had stepped into the position of assistant in chemistry without having obtained his doctorate, had just been relieved of his office.

Meanwhile Mother had taken a position in the Bloomington city schools as teacher of drawing in order that we might not be wholly dependent upon her parents. This teaching, together with housework and the care of a considerable flower and vegetable garden, was a heavy drain upon her time and strength.

Throughout this period the household was run by my grandmother with the help of our Negro cook, Lizzie Breckenridge, who served our family nearly fifty years.

My grandmother was a cheery, confident, practical person. She was never much interested in books, but all the family came to her with their aches and pains and cuts and bruises. We considered her to be as good as a doctor. She was, as I remember her, a charming hostess, witty and tactful and resourceful. I do not recall ever seeing her sick except as she faded away toward the end of her one hundred and one years.

Lizzie came of a family of slaves who had been freed before

[2] Woodburn, *op. cit.*, p. 375.

the Civil War. Their presence in Bloomington was due to the Covenanter sympathy with the Negroes and she herself was a devout member of the Old Side Covenanter Church on South Walnut Street. She was a student of the stars, a study to which my grandfather had introduced her. She knew all the principal constellations and all the brighter stars, and no comet ever escaped her attention. A finer spirit there never was. We all looked upon her as one of the family.

Looking back over this period, the picture of my grandfather occupies always an important place. In the earlier years I see him at his desk upstairs, toiling over the history of the University, which, with a small honorarium, had been assigned to him in lieu of a pension. He was slightly below average in height, brisk in his movements, always neatly dressed, to the end of his days relying upon his Philadelphia tailor for his clothing. He was an orderly person, keeping his papers neatly filed and his books carefully arranged. He would sometimes get mildly irritated if I misplaced his woodworking or drawing instruments, but he encouraged me to use them, and he was never too busy to help me with a problem in mathematics or a passage in Latin. I do not remember at any time any disagreements between him and my grandmother. She ran the household, and he did not interfere. But he was its head. We all recognized that.

My schooling, as may be inferred, was considerably delayed. I had been held back by reason of the transfer from Lawrenceville, and I was still further delayed because of an injury to my left eye, which occurred shortly before my eighth birthday in 1884.

I can remember quite well how it happened. At dinner that day the conversation had turned to the reaction of winking. My grandfather spoke of its protective function, and I left the table, curious about it all, and went to the front yard. There I began to swing on a gate underneath a large pear tree full of ripening pears. Two boys came along and demanded some pears. I refused. Thereupon one of them aimed a toy gun at me, one of the type that carried a rubber contraption on a wooden stock. Half curiously, half defiantly, I resolved not to wink. He banged away, and I was struck by an iron nail directly in the pupil of the eye. The eyelid was not touched.

Expert care for such an injury was hard to find at that time in southern Indiana, but it so happened that one of my grandfather's former students had become a distinguished oculist. This man, Dr. Williams, lived in Cincinnati, and my grandfather wrote to him. He did this the more confidently in that Dr. Williams in his student days had been the central figure in a heated controversy and my grandfather had championed him. It seems that the faculty was having a party one evening at the home of Dr. James F. Dodds, and the president, in accordance with the custom on rainy days in that period, took off his boots and left them just outside the door. A group of students on the prowl spied those boots, placed them on a pole and executed a dance around them. This was regarded by a majority of the faculty as a serious affront, and an apology was demanded. Two of the students, one of them the future oculist, refused to apologize and were expelled. They went then to Asbury University, or De Pauw, as it is now called.[3] It was to this man that I was sent in care of my grandmother. He was not able

[3] Woodburn, *op. cit.* p. 129, reports an exodus from Asbury to Indiana in 1855, but he makes no mention of this incident. For this reason he misses the point of T. A. Wylie's notation on the margin of the faculty record-book that the Indiana faculty's action in receiving the recalcitrant students was prompted by "a little spirit of revenge." One of the students involved in the exodus from Asbury was Robert R. Hitt, later a distinguished congressman from Illinois.

to save the sight of the eye. Its loss may have had an adverse effect upon my skill on the ballfield and the tennis court, but I have not been aware of the difference.

The visit to Cincinnati, the brief sojourn in Dr. Williams's palatial home in the Walnut Hills section overlooking the river, and the three-week sojourn in Newport in the home of an aunt by marriage and her mother, Mrs. James Thompson, I can remember very well. The latter was a cousin of Professor Nathaniel Shaler, the geologist, whose mother lived just across the street.

For the remainder of the preschool period my memory is hazy. As nearly as I can recall, I spent much of my time playing with my blocks, daubing paint over Kate Greenaway girls, and drawing pictures of railway trains and engines. Even before I could read I took great delight in *St. Nicholas,* with its stories and pictures. *Swiss Family Robinson* was my favorite book.

So it came to pass that I was well past my eighth birthday at the time I entered the first grade at midyear. However, I had had some instruction from my father earlier, and school was easy for me. I was soon promoted to the second grade. Later on I skipped the fifth grade. Usually I ranked first or second in the class, a fact of which I was somewhat ashamed. At least in the higher grades I sensed the fact that the other boys did not approve of scholastic proficiency.

My sister, who has been an important factor in my life, was an extremely bright and active youngster with a keen sense of humor. At the age of eight she started writing verses, some of which were very clever. In that same year, 1887, she established a record in an intelligence test given in the city schools. This test consisted of a series of errors which the pupils were to correct. My sister, then in the third grade, made a perfect score and was the only one in all eight grades who made a perfect score. William Lowe Bryan, a pioneer in intelligence testing and later president of Indiana University, who gave the test, has told me many times of her performance. He was quite impressed by it. With all her brilliance she was at the same time an outgoing, attractive child, unusually free from malicious tendencies, and I cannot recall any clashes between us, except perhaps for a good-natured joke at my expense.

With the exception of two or three friends I do not recall having had much to do with other youngsters outside of the home circle until my eleventh year. I then became a more or less regular member of the gang made up mostly from the "gown" element in that college town. I played on their baseball and football teams, but I was no shining light.

It may be of interest to note that the real leader of our gang, Oscar Perry, was never so recognized. Oscar was a capable, attractive fellow, fertile in ideas, well-supplied with self-confidence and really skillful in the various sports. Most of our meetings were held in his father's barn. In spite of these qualifications, he was never elected captain either of the baseball or football teams. For this his undersized twin brother was chiefly responsible. He electioneered against him. His usual argument was this: "You know, Oscar would kinda like to be captain. But really it would not be good for him. He's too stuck on himself already." That argument always carried. But Oscar took it in good part. Later on, in college, he was elected captain of the varsity football team. He became a very successful mining engineer.

One thing I did not do was to study music. Mother could have taught me to play the piano, but I was not interested. Music was frowned on by our gang as being "girls' business," and Mother did not believe in bringing pressure to bear.

The name I went by among the gang was "Fessor." There was nothing distinctive about this. I was called "Fessor" for the same reason the doctor's son was called "Doc." During this period I was rather shy and distrustful of myself. I was fond of books, fond also of working with tools. After school I usually went home rather than off with the others. I had chores to do, wood to split and carry up, the garden to care for and the chickens to feed. And there were many interesting things to do, especially in my grandfather's workshop.

In the matter of religion I was brought up rather strictly. My grandfather was a faithful Scotch-Irish Covenanter. Every Sunday morning, regardless of weather, he made his way to church and sat in the family pew, two seats from the front, and we all went with him. Until my ninth year, we went to the United Presbyterian Church. But in 1885 the old Wylie Memorial Church in Philadelphia joined the Philadelphia Presbytery, and my grandfather, as a matter of family loyalty, put in his letter with the Presbyterian church which is "neither Reformed nor United." The family church in Philadelphia had been independent since 1869 in consequence of the Synod's action in excommunicating its leading layman, Mr. George H. Stuart, for the "sin of occasional hearing." By that is meant visiting other churches and joining with their congregations in singing other hymns than the Psalms of David, a practice he had begun while serving as president of the Christian Commission during the Civil War,[4] and had refused to discontinue.

This transfer did not, however, mean any change in our be-

[4] The Christian Commission during the Civil War was an interchurch organization corresponding somewhat to the Young Men's Christian Association of World War I. For a consideration of the psalm-singing Presbyterians see my *Religion in Crisis and Custom* (New York: Harper & Brothers, 1955), chap. ii; also my "Divided Protestantism in a Midwest County," *Journal of Religion,* Vol. 20: No. 4, October, 1940, 359-81.

liefs and practices. Family prayers were held every morning and every evening, and on Sundays we were not supposed to do any whistling or any reading except that which was definitely religious. With all his strictness in these matters, my grandfather was a gentle and kindly man with considerable breadth of view, and none of us resented his requirements.

"HALFWAY LONG PANTS"

Six years after we had returned to the old home our household was considerably enlarged. Uncle Brown Wylie died, leaving four minor children, and the three youngest came to live with their grandparents. This was no light responsibility for a woman of seventy-eight, but my grandmother accepted it with her characteristic cheerfulness.

I was at this time in the first year of high school. Although fourteen years old I was still in knickerbockers, but it was not long before I began to aspire to the dignity of long trousers. Mother gently opposed this idea. She did not want me to grow up too rapidly. In the resulting difference of opinion my grandmother suggested a compromise. Why not "halfway long pants"? Her suggestion was not followed, but I have long looked upon it as furnishing an appropriate symbol for this particular period, at least in my own life.

At this time I took myself with extreme seriousness and I suffered tortures in consequence. When finally I did don the coveted symbol of manhood—a garment which did actually before many months find its way above my shoe-tops—my frivolous young sister celebrated the occasion with some scurrilous verses which caused me to writhe with wounded dignity. All the way through high school the changes and adjustments incidental to growth were attended with like discomforts.

I am not sure that it would be correct to speak of any scholastic aspirations during this period, for I was halting between two opinions. On the one hand was the opinion of the "bunch" that it was not good form to get marks that were too high. On the other hand was a desire to excel in a field in which I was best adapted. Actually I did neither the one nor the other. I stood second at the end of my senior year in high school. My favorite study at this time was mathematics. This was not because of any unusual ability along that line. In the grades I used to hate arithmetic. But it so happened that by dint of much effort I succeeded on several occasions in solving problems that no one else in the class had solved. The words of commendation which I received on these occasions were pleasing to my ears and I began to get interested in algebra. In geometry I was still more interested. But English I hated. At least, I did not like to write, and English literature was for me a vague and tedious thing. I did like grammar. In Latin I was only fair, owing largely to the fact that I used to go to my grandfather for help, and thus I failed to develop any proficiency of my own.

It was chiefly in my social relations that I had difficulty. In the grades I had been shy and distrustful of myself, more at home with my books or in the workshop than with my schoolmates. This tendency became accentuated in high school. On Friday afternoons, the period which in those days was reserved for declamations and speeches, I suffered severely from stage fright. Even in the classroom I had spasms of timidity. Also among other boys I felt insecure. I found my greatest satisfaction in the companionship of a few friends. During my first year in high school and part of my second year, my special chum was the son of one of the college professors. He lived on the opposite side of the town, but I spent a good bit of time at his house, and he at mine. We made expeditions together out into the country in search of butterflies or hickory nuts or whatever the season offered. We went together to baseball and football games and we experimented in woodworking. I do not recall that we discussed girls or sex matters except incidentally.

During the second year in high school the stamp-collecting craze struck town. That was in 1891-92. In Bloomington no one had collected stamps before, and we had a glorious time ransacking attics. One great find was in the attic of an old foundry where rifles had been made for the Union Army during the Civil War. Here we found stamps of large denominations in great abundance. One of our group came from a missionary family. His parents had lived in China twenty-five or thirty years before and had a store of valuable stamps. I had our attic where my grandfather had carefully filed away his old letters, envelopes and all, going back before the time stamps were first introduced. Into this enterprise I was initiated by this friend of mine, who had already become familiar with the game. Early in my searches I chanced upon a valuable stamp, a United States three-cent stamp of the 1840's made from an unusual die. My friend suggested a trade. I consented, and traded to him a stamp listed at fifteen dollars for one listed at fifteen cents. When I discovered what had happened I took it rather hard.

During this period I became much interested in physical culture. I invested in a pair of dumbbells. I made a pair of Indian clubs on my grandfather's turning lathe, and spent hours twirling them; I would take deep breaths and raise myself up and down on my toes; I would go to the quarry near our home and throw stones by the hundred. During my second year in high school we were given the privilege of using the University gymnasium three times a week. Of this I availed myself to the full. I never became proficient on the diamond or the gridiron, but I was at least above average in strength.

With girls I was ill at ease. I did not learn to dance. This was not due to religious scruples, but rather to the fact that my closest friends did not dance. With my sister's friends I had few dealings. They were only "kids," not yet in their teens.

Concerning sexual problems my memories of the high school period merge into those of later years. It is only necessary at this point to say that there was plenty of stress and that the "facts of life" were explained to me somewhat belatedly by a book mother gave me, telling what adolescent boys ought to know. I also did some surreptitious exploration of my own in Rees's Encyclopedia and in some medical books. The trouble was not in lack of knowledge. I knew enough. In fact the information thus obtained became itself a source of difficulty. It remained something fascinating and terrifying about which I was afraid to talk. I know that serious difficulty began at this time, but it is difficult for me to separate this period from that of later adolescence in which I shall consider it more in detail.

I was a regular attendant at the Presbyterian church, to which our family belonged. Attendance at this church was made easier by the fact that most of our "crowd" also belonged there. Dr. George N. Luccock was at that time the pastor, and President John Merle Coulter of the University and his family were regular attendants. During my second year in high school the evangelist, Wilbur Chapman, held a series of meetings in Bloomington, and along with four or five others of our group I joined the church. Although taken under revivalistic influences, this step involved no special religious experience. I assented at once when asked, waiting only to be sure that I was really eligible. I also joined the Christian Endeavor Society, and on Sunday evenings in great distress of mind I would read a verse of scripture or some pious sentiment, as the pledge required. There were at no time any intellectual difficulties. The faith of my fathers was, for me, at one with the authority of science.

In the warfare between science and religion which waged so furiously during the later nineteenth century, my grandfather may have been on the conservative side. If so, he made no issue of it. I know that he accepted the scientific account of the age of the earth. I do not know his attitude on the theory of evolution. Apparently he did not permit his scientific views to interfere with his loyalty to his church. My father, however, had not been able to accept Bloomington's brand of Presbyterianism. Later on he had joined the Congregational church and on that occasion he wrote out a statement of belief which shows that he was a thoroughgoing liberal. This I knew from my mother, who rather early in her life had accepted the liberal position. My own problems were therefore not theological. They had to do with my inner adjustments.

UNDERGRADUATE DAYS

The memories of my undergraduate days in college are even more painful to me than those of the high school period. It was a time of unrest, of social maladjustment, and of failure to achieve any particular distinction.

During my high school period I had never felt sure of my status among other boys. This sense of insecurity was now greatly intensified by the fact that I received no invitation to join the fraternity to which my best friends belonged. To be sure, I was "spiked" by two good fraternities, and one of these I actually joined, but I took part only halfheartedly. I attended some of the dances and made a few feeble attempts to learn the art of dancing, but I was still ill at ease with girls. At least, I had no success in establishing friendly relations with the girls who were attractive to me.

In my first year in college I went out for football, but I was a long way off from making the team. In the winter I devoted myself to handball, and I continued this interest throughout my college course. I found my chief satisfactions in the associations formed on the tennis court. Rather early in the college period I made a tennis court of my own on the five-acre place which my grandfather owned, and I found many who were glad to use it. One of my happiest relationships was with Professor John A. Bergstrom, an experimental psychologist of great promise, who lived across the street from us. He was one of the best tennis players I have known, not showy, but steady and careful, and a student of the game. His skill is evidenced by the fact that over a period of nine years of steady playing, no one ever succeeded in winning a single set from him. He was called to Stanford shortly after the turn of the century, and died a few years later.

From early years I had heard much from my mother about "Arbutus Hill." This hill, which lay five miles east of town, was associated with my father's memory. It was he who had discovered it, and the trailing arbutus, from which it took its name, had been adopted as the college flower. This hill was believed to be the only place in the state where arbutus grew, and every spring scores of people visited the hill and brought back a few little sprays. While still in first-year high school, I had joined these pilgrims, and I continued to go there every spring. During my second year in college I found my first new hill. I shall never forget that day. The arbutus was out in all its glory. Never before nor since have I found anything that looked to me more beautiful. I had been there only a few minutes when a carriage made its appearance on the opposite slope, and Dr. William Lowe Bryan, our professor of philosophy and psychology, got out. He was much surprised to see me and wanted to know how I had found the place. He then suggested that we keep it secret in order to protect the flowers.

It was veneration for my father that determined my choice of a major subject in the college course. After completing the required courses in English, German, and mathematics, I was having a hard time deciding what to take as my specialty. I thought seriously of mathematics, but I eventually decided upon German, chiefly because my father had been a teacher of modern languages. With this decision made, I threw myself vigorously into my chosen field, taking also Greek and French and then, in my senior year, Gothic and Old English.

Of great importance in my development was a course I took in my sophomore year under Professor Bryan. This was a course in ethics, which was considered the best course in the University, even as Dr. Bryan himself was looked upon as our greatest teacher. I became deeply interested in, also somewhat bewildered at, the vast universe it opened before me. Most important for me was the fact that Dr. Bryan used my father as an exemplification of the great teacher, speaking particularly of his belief in the necessity of prompt punishment and of his recognition of the need for encouragement and consistency. This greatly intensified my devotion to his memory and reinforced the idealism which was one of the components in the conflict and unrest of this period.

On June 9, 1895, my grandfather died after a lingering illness. Two days later, his old colleague Daniel Kirkwood passed away in California. Both men had belonged to what was known as Indiana University's "Big Four."[5] Kirkwood was a forerunner of the new day in higher education. He was a specialist in mathematical astronomy. Although without access to telescopes or other astronomical instruments, he had worked out original and significant theories regarding comets, meteors, nebulae, and planetary movements, which had won recognition across the ocean where he was known as "the Kepler of America." The others of the old guard were Elisha Ballantine, a Presbyterian minister of liberal views and a fine Greek scholar, and Richard Owen, son of Robert Owen, who as a boy had come over from Scotland with New Harmony's "boat-load of knowledge." During the Civil War, Richard Owen had been for some time commander of the Union prison at Camp Morton, and the University now cherishes a statue of him erected in 1913 by his one-time Confederate prisoners in recognition of his kindly treatment of them. In order to secure him for the University my grandfather had given up his own chair of natural philosophy and had taken that of Latin and Greek, an arrangement which held for three years. He then resumed the chair of natural philosophy, and Professor Owen took over geology and chemistry and German and French. It was Professor Owen who brought my father to the University. Of the "Big Four," I think of my grandfather as perhaps the most distinctive representative of the old order with its classical learning and its rock-ribbed devotion to age-old religion and morality. As such he had been recognized with the honorary degree of doctor of divinity by Princeton, Miami, and Monmouth, and with that of doctor of laws by the University of Pennsylvania.

A year after my grandfather's death, Uncle Arthur Mellette,

[5] Woodburn, *op. cit.*, pp. 342-358.

who had been governor of South Dakota, also passed away not long after losing all his property—no inconsiderable amount—because of a defaulting state treasurer on whose bond he had gone. These deaths removed the last of the significant men in the family, and left me feeling the pressure of a situation to which I was unequal.

The sense of inadequacy was perhaps increased when in 1896 my sister entered college. She was received with open arms and was "rushed" vigorously by both the leading sororities. I was proud of her, but I was reminded of my own deficiencies. Through her I had contacts with the other sex, but I was still awkward, and the painful shyness of the high school period was still in evidence. I had to force myself when it came to speaking in public, even in the classroom. I attended social affairs from a sense of duty, not because I found any satisfaction in them.

It is only with difficulty that I am able to recall the steps in the development of the inner conflict which has given me so much trouble. I seldom discussed the subject of sex with other boys, not even with my most intimate friends, and I had little dealing with girls. But all the while I was extremely sensitive on the subject, and the entire realm of sex was for me at once fascinating and terrifying. The essence of the difficulty lay thus in the fact that these sexual interests could neither be controlled nor acknowledged for fear of condemnation. Because of the presence of instinctual cravings which to me were forbidden, I felt isolated from my fellows. That, as I see it, is the explanation of the grave social maladjustments of this period—the shyness, the self-consciousness, the anxiety. I was never any good at bluffing. When I did wrong, I always got caught.

It may be noted that I did not permit myself to read the ordinary obscene stuff or to look at the vulgar cards which the boys sometimes passed around. What I did was to turn to certain parts of the Bible, to certain plays of Shakespeare, and to certain articles in the encyclopedias, deceiving myself with the idea that I was seeking after knowledge. Such temptations were increased when, as a specialist in languages, I was free to browse around in the departmental library. Certain French novels had an influence upon me which was far from wholesome, not necessarily because these books were "bad," but because they dealt frankly with emotionally charged problems. They added fuel to fire that was already more than I could control.

Most vividly do I remember one occasion when I undertook to burn out the caterpillars in a walnut tree in our orchard. I used a long pole capped on the end with rags soaked in kerosene. With this I did considerable damage to the caterpillars. When I had finished, I laid the pole down on the ground. A little later I came back, inspected the pole, and leaned it up against the woodhouse. Then I went to my room and buried myself in Tolstoi's *Anna Karenina*. This was for me in that period of my life the kind of reading which was equivalent to playing with fire, but I permitted myself to read it, especially in vacations, because it was something which men of culture ought to be acquainted with. I can recall the feeling which had come over me from the reading, a sort of vertigo, when suddenly I heard the cry of "fire!" It did not take long to discover what the trouble was. Our woodhouse was on fire! Thanks to prompt action on the part of the city fire department, the fire was put out with only moderate loss, and the house itself did not catch fire. Enough of the woodhouse remained to show how the fire started. It had come from the pole which I had put up against the building. Rather symbolic, it seemed to me, of my personal situation. This happened, I believe, in the vacation preceding my senior year.

With the ending of the college course in 1897, I was twenty years old, the youngest in the class as to chronological age and still younger in the matter of maturity. I was unsure of myself, and at the same time possessed of exalted ideas and intent upon finding a high school teaching position at the very least. But no job presented itself which I was willing to accept. Indiana's President Swain suggested a country school. He thought it would be a valuable experience for me, but I scorned the idea.

A NEW START

The failure to find employment immediately after graduation was a terrific blow to me. However, I had a good idea of where the trouble lay and I set to work at putting my house in order. I began that task by fixing up my room and raising the standards of caring for it. I also undertook the care of our garden and did a really good job. I followed through a course of reading and study, and I began to give attention to my handwriting, which had been unformed and changeable. I tried to work out a style of my own modeled somewhat after that of an English teacher for whom I felt a considerable liking. At the end of the summer I enrolled in the graduate school.

During the fall of 1897 things went well. I entered the new school year with a sense of virtue because of the vigorous work of the summer. I got a job as desk attendant in the University library and I became deeply interested in my studies, especially in the reading of William James's *Principles of Psychology* under the guidance of Dr. Bryan. I also took a course in experimental psychology under Dr. Bergstrom, and more German, more

French, more Greek. Not without importance was the Bible class I attended at the United Presbyterian Church under Dr. Bryan.

All went well until the Christmas vacation. Then came a fall from grace. I read a novel of Zola's, one of the kind I could not assimilate, and I crossed the line I had determined not to cross.[6] As a result I felt stripped of self-respect and burdened with a heavy sense of failure and guilt. It was in this mood that I entered the new quarter of study.

As the quarter advanced the inner tension increased. We were reading Professor James's chapters on "Habit" and "Will." These did not bring me any comfort. Then, if my memory serves me aright, we had that winter a visit from Colonel Francis Parker of Chicago, one of the recognized educational leaders of the country and an old friend of my father's. In the course of his lecture he made some pointed remarks about abuse of the imagination. When at the close I went up with Mother to speak to him, he remarked that my father was the greatest teacher he had ever known and that William T. Harris had said the same thing. Here, then, was the touching of a sore spot by a man who represented my father. It intensified the idealistic component and at the same time made me aware of my shortcomings.

Toward spring I received a letter from my great-uncle in Philadelphia, the brother of my grandfather and the pastor of the old Wylie Memorial Church, inquiring about my "spiritual condition." Meanwhile I had made an alarming discovery. As I turned the leaves of my Greek dictionary, obscene words would

[6] The "transgression" referred to was that of a psychically induced orgasm. Concerning my problem, I may say that it had to do chiefly with erotic fantasy derived for the most part from reading. Actual orgasm was not frequent, and when it did occur it resulted usually from psychic stimulation. The fantasies were always of the opposite sex.

leap out of its pages and hit me in the eye; and so they would leap out of other dictionaries also. It was obvious that something was seriously wrong.

The tension reached the breaking point on Easter morning of 1898. I got up early that morning after a sleepless night and went out into the garden where Mother's hyacinths and daffodils were in full bloom. It was a beautiful day, but there was no sunshine there for me, and no beauty—nothing but black despair. I came back to my room and threw myself on my knees with an agonized call for help. And help came! Something seemed to say to me almost in words, "Don't be afraid to tell."

With this it seemed as though a great burden had been taken away. I felt very happy. That day I had a talk with Mother. What I said and what she said I do not remember. She understood. That was enough. Then I felt impelled to go to Dr. Bryan. I talked with him under the trees at his home on North College Avenue. I cannot remember much of that talk either, but one thing stands out clear. He told me that it would always be necessary to fight for control of the instincts and that I must look to Christ for help, and to some good woman.

Following that Easter Sunday I found myself unable to do the routine classwork. Only what was related to my dominant interests could hold my attention. My mind was in a tumult, surging with all sorts of ideas, ideas which came from many sources, vivid memories from out of the past, especially from the period of childhood, and others which seemed to come from no previous experience of my own. There were even ideas of having lived before and of being more important than I had ever dreamed. But I was hopeful, happy, confident.

Within a few days I was approached by one of the Young Men's Christian Association secretaries with the invitation to take a Bible study group. This I accepted at once, looking upon it as a divine leading. In this new task I found real satisfaction. I also made some false moves, chiefly in the nature of attempts to talk of personal religion with some of my friends.

What I did during the following summer vacation I cannot distinctly remember. I think I brushed up on my Latin by taking a college course. I know I did much reading in the field of religion. In any case, the following fall I found myself with a job as teacher of German and French in the Bloomington High School.

In trying to understand what happened to me on that Easter morning in 1898 and during the year that followed I get much help from a theory which is known as "Bryan's Law of the Plateaus in Learning." This theory, advanced by the beloved teacher who has had such an important part in my life, was based upon a study of the rate of learning in telegraphy. It was found that in the acquisition of skill, the curve of progress showed a tendency to strike certain levels and stay there, perhaps even to drop a little, until suddenly there would come an abrupt upward turn which would continue for a time with diminishing acceleration until again a dead level was found. These plateaus were more marked in receiving messages than in sending them, but they were present in both. The explanation was found in the hypothesis that at the point where the dead level is reached some obstruction is encountered, and at the point where the sharp upward turn occurs this obstacle is removed or overcome.

The application seems clear. My development had been checked by the presence of instinctual claims which could be neither controlled nor acknowledged for fear of condemnation. The prompting, "Do not be afraid to tell," brought relief by socializing the difficulty, and it did so on the level of what for me was abiding and universal. I was now at one with the internalized fellowship of the best, the fellowship which is represented by the idea of God. I felt now like a new being. There was new hope and new confidence, and the painful shyness which so long had troubled me seemed to have disappeared. At least, I felt a freedom in my association with others which I had not felt before; I found new interest in my work, and increased effectiveness.

Since my high school teaching was only a part-time job, I took additional work in German and French at the University. I became especially interested in the French courses because of the new head of the department, Professor Kuersteiner, who had just arrived on the scene. I liked him and I liked his methods of teaching, and under his guidance and that of Professor Karsten of the German department, I gave especial attention to philology.

For my effectiveness as a teacher in the high school I can make no great claim. I had difficulty, especially in the matter of discipline. Nevertheless, as a result of the work done at the University, new opportunities presented themselves. I was offered an instructorship in German at Vanderbilt University in Nashville, Tennessee, and a position as tutor in French at Indiana University. I chose the latter.

Now for the first time I found myself enjoying friendly relationships with young women. This I attribute to the release from the diffidence of the earlier years, also to the fact that my sister was now at the height of her popularity in college. She was editor-in-chief of the college annual, the *Arbutus*, as it was called, president of her sorority, and voted the best-liked girl in college.

Again my memory is hazy and I cannot recall the course of events. The important fact is that with the passing of time I became less watchful, and the old enemy got hold of me again. During the early part of 1902, I grew increasingly restless. I was aware of the fact that it was time for me to take decisive action of some sort. If I were to continue as a teacher of languages, I should be getting further training. I was also aware of the danger within, and fearful of my ability to win out in what was for me a temptation-laden situation. Since in French literature I was constantly confronted with the unassimilated sex problem, a change of occupation seemed called for.

This increasing unrest eventuated in the decision to give up my career as a teacher of languages and to embark upon a new course, that of a forester. Regarding this decision, I can say that it was entirely free. I had already been advanced to an instructorship in romance languages, and both Professor Kuersteiner and President Bryan had assured me of a leave of absence to study abroad.

Like others of my major decisions, this decision to study forestry came automatically. I had for some days been feeling especially tense and restless, when I chanced upon an article on forestry as a profession. I read it only in part, and then went out in considerable excitement, feeling that the way was clear and the decision made.

While apparently sudden, this decision had its explanation in interests of long standing. I have reference to my activities in exploring the wide stretches of woodland east of Bloomington in search of trailing arbutus. This flower has thus far defied all attempts at cultivation, but I had succeeded in discovering the conditions under which it grew. I had found that in this area it was likely to be found on steep western exposures in shale formations and that it grew in close association with partridgeberry, wintergreen, huckleberry, and moss under a broken stand of oak and hickory. It was therefore easy to find new places, and I had by this time found ten new arbutus-covered hillsides.

This decision to become a forester, like my interest in the arbutus itself, thus grew out of a loyalty to my father's memory which had become one with my religion. I can still remember the tense emotion which marked that period, emotion in which the thought of him was dominant. I vowed that I would be true to the heritage he had left me. This decision stood also for the idea of adventure, of exploration, of cutting loose from the beaten path and starting forth into unknown territory. Not only in retrospect have I had this feeling. That was my feeling then.

III

THE CALL TO THE
MINISTRY

BORDERS OF THE PROMISED LAND

IT WAS AFTER I had made the decision to become a forester that I met Alice Batchelder. She was an Easterner, a native of Portsmouth, New Hampshire, and a graduate of Smith College, who came to Indiana University in 1902 as Secretary of the Young Women's Christian Association. I saw her for the first time at a convocation, where she was introduced to the student body and made a brief address. She was at that time twenty-two years of age. She was somewhat above average height, with wavy hair of a genuine golden color. What she said I do not remember, but she spoke in a clear, well-modulated voice, and I was impressed with her sincerity and earnestness. I fell in love with her then and there. It was a one-sided affair, a love that swept me off my feet. I received little encouragement, but I saw her from time to time as often as she would let me. In the spring I took her out driving several times, once to my favorite arbutus-carpeted hillside, another time to Cedar Bluff in search of shooting star and columbine. It was at Cedar Bluff that I told her of my love for her, asking at least for her friendship. She was very gentle in her answer, but it was not the one I longed for. She felt it best that our relationship should cease entirely.

At the close of the year we both left Bloomington, she to become State Secretary of the Young Women's Christian Association in Missouri, I to join a forestry party on the eastern shore of Maryland. There I spent the summer thinking of her as I counted rings on bald cypress and loblolly pine or helped to run strip surveys through Worcester County's timberland. I found myself unable to give her up, and I had the deep feeling that my very existence was involved. I was having a hard fight to keep wayward erotic ideation under control. I promised myself that if I could keep the record clear for three months, then at the end of that time I would write to her. This I did, and I wrote telling her of my continued thought of her. But I received no answer. This was a severe blow and I did not know what to do. I recognized that she meant what she had said. Was it fair either to her or to myself to keep on hoping?

One evening as I was wrestling with the question of what to do, I resorted, as desperate men sometimes will, to what I regarded as rank superstition. I took my Bible and opened it at random. My eye fell upon the words, "Ask and ye shall receive, seek and ye shall find, knock and it shall be opened unto you. For every one that asketh receiveth; and he that seeketh findeth; and to him that knocketh it shall be opened." I was startled because this passage applied so directly to the problem on my mind.

The next night I tried the same thing. This time the words were these: "Therefore we ought to give the more earnest heed to the things that were heard, lest haply we drift away from them. For if the word spoken through angels proved steadfast and every transgression received a just recompense of reward, how shall we escape if we neglect so great salvation?" Here again, though not so clearly, I saw an answer to the question on my mind. In any case, the thought of her more and more took possession of me.

After the completion of my first year in the Yale Forest School the following June, I was assigned to the making of a working plan for a five-thousand-acre tract in southwestern New Hampshire under the leadership of Charles Lyford, an old Cornell stroke. This assignment I had requested because it sent me to Alice Batchelder's native state. In the late fall of 1904 a study of lumbering took me to the White Mountains of northern New Hampshire. On the way back I stopped off at Portsmouth, hoping to see her. It so happened that she was at home, but, calling unannounced, I met with a very chilly reception. I was heartbroken, and with a mind tense with despair I went on to Washington, where the Forest School men were to meet with the American Forestry Association.

In that state of mind I went on Sunday morning to the Church of the Covenant. The sermon that day was on the migration of Abraham. The main point in Dr. Hamlin's sermon, as it stands out in my memory, was the difference between following a certain course because of arbitrary desire and doing so in obedience to God's will. The man who starts out on a long and difficult quest in obedience to God's will must in the end reach his goal, whereas the man who is prompted by arbitrary desire can have no such assurance. Because of the tense and suggestible state of mind I was in that morning, this sermon could hardly have failed to have a profound effect. I took it as a message to me. It was followed by several sleepless nights.

The tense emotion did not subside with my return to New Haven. It was here toward Easter that the climax came. I was looking one evening through Emerson's essay on the "Oversoul," when my attention was arrested by the following passage:

The things that are really for thee gravitate to thee. You are running to seek your friend. Let your feet run, but your mind need not. If you do not find him, will you not acquiesce that it is best you should not find him? For there is a power which, as it is in you, is in him also, and could therefore very well bring you together, if it were for the best. You are preparing with eagerness to go and render a service to which your talent and your taste invite you, the love of men and the hope of fame. Has it not occurred to you, that you have no right to go unless you are equally willing to be prevented from going? O, believe, as thou livest, that every sound that is spoken over the round world, which thou oughtest to hear, will vibrate in thine ear! every proverb, every book, every byword that belongs to thee for aid or comfort shall surely come home through open or winding passages. Every friend whom not thy fantastic will, but the great and tender heart in thee craveth, shall lock thee in his embrace. And this because the heart in thee is the heart of all; not a valve, not a wall, not an intersection is there any where in nature, but one blood rolls uninterruptedly an endless circulation through all men, as the water of the globe is all one sea, and, truly seen, its tide is one.

These words seemed to apply to my situation. They helped to induce an attitude of resignation and trust, and thus brought peace to my troubled mind.

That night as I lay half awake, half asleep, something seemed to say to me just as on that Easter morning seven years before, "Write and tell her all about it." I arose almost mechanically and wrote to Alice, telling her of the moral struggle I had been having and of my reason for studying forestry.

After I had finished this letter, I began to question. Thinking then of the passage in Emerson and of the two passages of Scripture, I took the Bible again, and after a prayer I once more opened it at random. The verse I read was John 19:27—"Then said he to the disciple, 'Behold thy mother!'"

I was deeply moved, for regardless of its origin, this "message" pointed to what I was really seeking in Alice. I realized that my love for her was really a desperate cry for salvation and an appeal to a beloved person stronger than myself.

Shortly after sending the letter, while walking down New

Haven's Chapel Street, the idea came surging into my mind, "You have found the hills where the flowers grow. It must be your task to show the way to them."

This for me was the call to the ministry.

I had never before dreamed of such a step, for I had never seen in myself the qualifications requisite for that calling. I felt that I had no gift of expression, either in speech or in writing; neither did I have the personal qualities which a minister ought to have. But the idea seemed to carry authority because of the way it came. It also made sense. It meant that just as out of the devotion to my father's memory I had been led to discover new haunts of the flower that he loved, so now through that same devotion I had tapped anew the eternal sources of religious faith and renewal. It would also permit me to claim a place as a fellow worker with Alice. But still I questioned.

The next morning, April 2, was Sunday, and I went to Battell Chapel, on the Yale campus, where Henry Sloane Coffin was preaching. His theme was the Call to the Ministry. It seemed to be a message for me, and it set my doubts at rest. I then wrote two more letters to Alice, telling her of my decision, and voicing the hope that we might be able to serve together.

After the third letter had been sent there came, on April 9, another memorable sermon, one by Charles Cuthbert Hall, of Union Theological Seminary, also in Battell Chapel. His subject that morning was the ancient story of Abraham's sacrifice of Isaac. His theme was that before a man can enter into fellowship with God, he must endure some such test.

Three days later came the answer to my letters. Alice wrote that she had read my letters with much distress, that only one answer had ever been possible, and that she must ask me not to write to her any more or to think of her further. She would be afraid to say this if she did not know that higher than a man's love for a woman must be his love for God as the only motive to determine his conduct. I felt myself dashed to pieces. It was as if I had been trying to fly and had been brought crashing down. I gave way to a reaction of weakness and despair.[1]

With the close of the school year in 1905 I entered the Forest Service. For a full year I served with my chief of the previous summer in a forest survey of the state of New Hampshire. Following that I was assigned to the making of a working plan for the Henry's Lake National Forest just west of Yellowstone Park. I was then transferred to the Office of Silvics under Raphael Zon, the Forest Service's outstanding scientist, and assigned to the task of studying the commercial hickories. All of these assignments were full of interest, and in between each one came a sojourn in Washington, where under Chief Forester Gifford Pinchot and President Theodore Roosevelt, the Forest Service was going forward by leaps and bounds, and the conservation movement was getting under way.

All the while I kept thinking of Alice, and meditating on the call to the ministry which I believed I had received. After some two years had passed and I had paid off the indebtedness incurred in taking the forestry course, I began to consider the next step. But the way was not clear. It had been obscured, I felt, by my failure to stand the test which had followed the call.

I had already become somewhat worked up in my efforts to get clear on this problem when I went one Sunday evening to hear Dr. Woodrow, who had just accepted the call to the First Congrega-

[1] The reaction referred to here was physiologically that of emission without erection. It occurred three times in rapid succession. This was something which had not previously been a problem with me, but it left me now with a horrible sense of failure and guilt, especially in the light of Dr. Hall's sermon three days before. Psychologically, it was the collapse of faith, which left me at the mercy of ideas of despair and self-pity.

tional Church in Washington. His sermon I shall never forget. His subject was the "Broken Vessel." He ended by saying, "If, by chance, there is someone here tonight who has had a great vision of God's purpose for him and who has been unfaithful to that vision, I call upon him to arise and give himself into the hands of the Great Potter in order that he may be made again another vessel as it seemeth good unto the Potter."

This sermon had the effect of driving me nearly psychotic. I cannot remember what followed. I do know that I wrote to Alice, telling her of my steady purpose to enter the ministry and of the great perplexity in which I found myself by reason of my failure to stand the test two years before. This letter may have come to her at an opportune time. I have never been sure, but at least it has been my impression that she had been a Student Volunteer and that shortly before my letter came she had received word of her rejection for foreign service because of her health. However that may be, she now consented to see me.

The meeting took place at the Baptist Training Institute in Philadelphia early in the winter of 1908, and it served to clear the way for me. At the close she offered prayer in my behalf, asking for wisdom and guidance. I remember being in tears at the close of this prayer and kissing the hand she offered me. She responded by saying, "God's promises always come true."

I proceeded then with my plans and made arrangements to enter Union Theological Seminary in the fall, choosing that school because Dr. Coffin and President Hall were both connected with it. To this change of course, my mother gave her full consent and helped to make it possible.

I then wrote to Alice, telling her of my action, and because I had taken her closing words in Philadelphia as a virtual promise, given out of pity rather than out of love, I told her that I would never accept from her anything she could not give freely. She replied, saying that I must have misunderstood. She had given no promise. Her first answer had been final and could not be changed.

I went then into an abnormal condition which I can recall only hazily. I saw myself, as it were, in the thick of a great fight. I had been entrusted with a responsibility on which everything depended, but I had fallen and could not rise. Then I saw her, and it seemed that she had appeared and reappeared through the centuries. And always across her path stood a poor wretch whose claim of need could not be denied, one who for her was a heavy cross. She was therefore always lonely and sad. Then it came to me that even though I had fallen, even though I was a broken vessel, I might give her to someone else. And another man, one of my fellow foresters, seemed pointed out. I went to him and stumblingly asked him to accept this trust; and he seemed to understand. After that I was very happy. It seemed that the fight was won. Then came terrible darkness. I was horrified at the breach of conventionality of which I had been guilty. I must surely be insane. And yet this prompting had seemed to carry authority just like that of the Easter experience in 1898 and that of the call to the ministry in 1905.

In this time of turmoil before I had left Washington to enter Union, I felt impelled to start a Bible class at the boardinghouse on Sixteenth near M Street, where some twenty or thirty Forest Service men were taking their meals. This went awfully against the grain for me, but I had to do it, so it seemed. It will be clear that I was in this period at least near-psychotic, and that such behavior today would surely land me in St. Elizabeth's. In that day, however, some of my friends, deeply troubled though they were, stood by me. Among these I have reason to be especially grateful to my chief, Raphael Zon. But desperately uncomfortable though it made me, I stuck it out with the Bible class until it was time to enter the seminary.

In the fall of 1908 I entered Union Theological Seminary in New York City for three of the happiest years of my life. Alice consented to correspond with me, and I was well received by the group.

Union Seminary at that time was located on Park Avenue between 69th and 70th Streets. It had a student body of about one hundred and seventy, and a faculty of about twelve. What impressed me at once was the caliber of these men and the warm, friendly spirit which prevailed. It was the time of Protestantism's greatest hopefulness, the time when that great leader in foreign missions, John R. Mott, was calling for the evangelization of the world in this generation, and this hopefulness was soberly reflected at Union. I found there just what I needed.

Although Union was one of the most forward-looking theological schools in the country, there was no provision in its curriculum for the consideration of the subject in which I was especially interested, the psychology of religion as interpreted by William James. That was true of our theological schools generally at that time. The study of the psychology of religion had arisen during the eighteen-nineties in the secular educational institutions, but even in 1908, six years after the appearance of James's great *Varieties of Religious Experience*, it had as yet found little place within the structure of theological education. However, at Union I was introduced to fields of study which I found of great interest, and I was encouraged to approach them from my own standpoint.

For my practical experience that first year I was assigned to the Spring Street Presbyterian Church on New York's lower

West Side, under the supervision of Herbert Bates. For the summer period I went to the Adirondacks under the Adirondack Mission Board. There I was given a little church in the open country three miles from the village of Santa Clara, a church in which Dr. Harry Emerson Fosdick had once served as student pastor. The community was an impoverished one. It had been dependent upon a big lumber mill, which had cut all the timber and then moved away, leaving it to shift for itself. My salary of twenty-five dollars a month and living expenses was paid almost entirely by the Mission Board. All that the people were accustomed to contribute was derived almost entirely from a church social held near the end of the summer. This seemed to me an unhealthy situation.

For this reason I made a proposal to my people. The church building was badly in need of paint. How would it be, I asked them, if we should use the money given by the Mission Board to pay for the painting, and raise the money for the pastor's salary by direct subscription? I offered to raise thirty of the needed seventy-five dollars by working as a laborer. My proposal was received with little enthusiasm, but most of the people were willing to humor their pastor. In consequence, I put in twenty-five days at hard labor, working on road or farm alongside of the men of my parish, and the budget was oversubscribed. I also applied some of my forestry training to the study of the parish. I made a map of the parish, showing the location of the homes. I also made a list of persons twelve years of age and older, together with a brief characterization of each one. The next summer I returned to Santa Clara in order to follow through along the same general line. This second summer, instead of painting the church, we put up sheds for the horses. I have often wondered since how much those sheds were used before the advent

of automobiles made them unnecessary. I have also in later years
had doubts about some of my tactics.

The second year at Union was chiefly memorable for me by
reason of the arrival of George Albert Coe as professor of religious education and psychology. I took all the courses he offered, and found them helpful and stimulating. On some important issues I could not agree with him. For me, faith in the
reality of mystical experience was fundamental. For Professor
Coe, it was something in the nature of a red flag. He had long
been leading a crusade against the excesses of middle western
revivalism and he was convinced that the mystic derives from
his mystical experience nothing he has not brought to it. Although I disagreed with his interpretation of mystical experience,
I found very great help in his courses. In later years his interest
in my project was something for which I am eternally grateful.

Throughout this period Alice was always uppermost in my
mind, and her letters meant a lot to me. However, as I look back,
I see that I did not make as much of the privilege of writing as
I might have. It seemed to me of first importance that I should
do good work in my studies. Therefore I did not respond affirma-
tively to her suggestion that we correspond in French, and I
did not devote to my letters the time and thought needed to
make them really worthwhile. My academic standing I brought
from an average of 83 in the first semester to 96 in the senior
year, and 93 for the entire three years. Meanwhile the old battle
for self-control seemed to be in hand. I felt therefore a certain
degree of self-satisfaction. On this account I felt more keenly
the fact that Alice would not permit me to see her and that her
letters were written on her official stationery. In any case, at the
end of my second year at Union she sent me an excellent picture
of herself, one which I have always treasured.

At Christmas in 1910 she visited me at the Seminary and I went with her to Lowell, Massachusetts, where she had been general secretary of the Young Women's Christian Association since 1909. One memorable evening we went together to the Boston Symphony. The next day, on a walk to the nearby town of Billerica, she told me that there was no other man and that she had decided to give her heart a chance. Beyond that she would not commit herself. I returned to New York in a very happy mood. My roommate, however, felt that Alice did not show the love for me he would have wished to see.

Concerning the next three months, my memory is rather hazy. I do know that I was faced with the problem which confronts most seminary graduates, that of finding a church which is ready to trust its fortunes into their hands. In this I was embarrassed by the fact that a pastorate without Alice's help was for me unthinkable, and yet she had given me no right to promise that.

I recall also that my hopes for the future centered upon a trip into the country to which she had given her consent. As soon as the arbutus came into bloom, we were to visit some of my old haunts in New Hampshire. For this I made elaborate plans. I intended to go up a day or two beforehand to look over the ground and find the most likely spots.

But Alice planned it otherwise. She had heard of a place nearby at Ponemah, New Hampshire, and in a somewhat belated letter, written on her official stationery, she vetoed my plan. What was more, she announced that a friend of hers would be coming with us. It was a letter that hurt, and I gave way to the same reaction of weakness which had followed the "call" at New Haven in 1905. In consequence, I went to Lowell with a wrong "set," or attitude. As I look back upon it now, I am reasonably sure that she was ready to give the answer I longed for more than all else in the world. This, at least, is true, that as we were returning from Ponemah, her friend left, by agreement I think, remarking as she did so that Alice looked like a bride with all those flowers.

Clearly it was time for me to speak, and I longed to do so and felt a deep tenderness come over me. But I was not ready and the words would not come. All that I did was to take her picture—twelve exposures! Then the friend returned, and the precious chance was gone.

I felt utterly miserable. How to account for it I do not know, but for the return trip I bought a ticket to Boston, where my sister was living, instead of to Lowell. I can still see the flash in Alice's eyes as she inquired whether she had heard correctly. When we pulled into Lowell, she would not let me accompany her. Looking back, I am sure she interpreted my ineptness as due to resentment on my part. I felt at the time as though an evil spirit had taken possession of me, but that spirit was not one of resentment. I was just feeling terribly uncomfortable and I wanted to get off by myself.

In any case I went back brokenhearted. As soon as possible I got on the telephone, and she consented to see me the next day. But nothing I was able to say could repair the damage. She gave her answer. Our friendship had brought happiness to neither of us, and she was sure that it was not God's will that it should continue.

On my return to the Seminary I wrote, begging for the privilege of seeing her again. She replied asking me not to write further, and stated that she would not see me again unless she decided to give me her love. I replied that I would not and could not give up until I was sure that the right ending had been reached.

How she felt I do not know. I have never flattered myself that anything in me could have caught her imagination, but in so far as she had believed in my love for her, she must have been deeply hurt. Years later she told me that she had lost her position as general secretary at Lowell. In view of her splendid efficiency and of the fact that she left Lowell only a few months after the Ponemah tragedy I cannot but wonder if her vocational setback must not be charged to my account.

Looking back, I have often wondered what difference it would have made in my life if I could have gone through the years with her. She was, as I saw her, a charming, highly gifted, level-headed woman with deep feelings and a high temper, which she kept under strict control. The key to her character I find in her statement to me that she had "decided to give her heart a chance." She had a New England conscience. She could always be counted on to do what she thought was right and to follow a consistent course regardless of her feelings. She always had a superior rating in her studies and she was very skillful with pen and brush. Of one thing I am sure. Any household of hers would have been well-ordered.

YEARS OF WANDERING

Fortunately for me, after graduating in 1911, I was given a challenging job; and in Fred Eastman, a brilliant younger classmate, I found a friend to whose understanding and loyalty I am forever indebted. Both of us had enlisted for country church work in response to an appeal by Dr. Warren H. Wilson of the Presbyterian Board of Home Missions. Just why we chose country churches is a fair question, for neither of us knew much about country life. In my own case it seemed a logical next step for a onetime forester. It was also in line with what I had been doing at Santa Clara. As for Fred, he had reacted against the scramble for strong churches which we had observed among some of our associates. In any case, Dr. Wilson made an impression on both of us, and since neither of us was married, the way seemed clear. We had been assigned to small churches in northeastern Missouri, when Dr. Wilson called us in. He had just been asked by the Kirksville Normal School to collaborate in a study of church and school conditions in that same section of Missouri to which we were going, and he was wondering if we might be interested in undertaking that study before tying ourselves down with churches.

As things turned out, the survey was a fortunate suggestion. Our churches failed to materialize. I was to have had a small church in the village of Ethel. I had assumed that since the Mission Board was to pay three-fifths of the thousand-dollar salary, there would be little question regarding the appointment. But I had reckoned without taking account of the rural mind. After preaching there, I was considerably nettled when word came that I would not do, and Fred subjected me to some good-natured chaffing over my inability to touch the popular heart. Meantime his own assignment had proved unsatisfactory because of serious overchurching in the community, and he was sent to Ethel. On his return, he reported that he had made quite a hit. Five days later word came that he would not do. The explanation was appended that neither of us was "intense" enough. This meant, we learned later, that we were not sufficiently versed in the gentle art of "drilling for water," that is, of eliciting tears.

Thus it came to pass that in June, 1911, we set forth on bicycles, each armed with a lengthy questionnaire dealing with all phases of rural economic, social, and religious life and with the distribution and activities of churches and schools. In order to find the answers to some of these questions, I drew upon my forestry experience and made use of the sample-plot method. I chose a number of representative school districts, and with the aid of trustworthy informants I made a list of persons over twelve years of age, together with information regarding their health, education, occupation, church affiliation, and church attendance. I also questioned the church leaders regarding what they were trying to do. Fred stuck more closely to the questionnaire. At the close of the summer we wrote up a report. My part in that report was in the form of pictures and statistical tables. Fred made use of his outstanding literary ability to write a report which was listened to with great interest at a church conference that fall. Later, in its printed form, it was widely read.

In the fall, following the Missouri survey, Fred was sent to Webster County, Kentucky, and then in the winter to Montgomery County, Maryland, to make similar surveys. I was sent to Gibson County in western Tennessee and after that to the Salt River Presbytery in Missouri. Both of us found this survey work a fine introduction to sociology and economics, and in Dr. Wilson we had an incomparable guide.

An outstanding feature of the situation revealed by our survey was the prevalence of the circuit-rider system. The rural and village churches in the regions we studied were served by absentee ministers who lived in the population centers and preached on Sundays once or twice a month in widely separated churches with whose people they had minimal acquaintance.

Significant also were the findings with reference to church attendance which I made at this time and supplemented later by studies in Kansas and in Maine. According to these findings, the influence of the church, as measured by church attendance, varies inversely with the degree of liberalization of popular religious opinion. Thus, in western Tennessee, where extreme conservatism held sway, only 20 per cent of the heads of families were classed by their neighbors as nonchurchgoers. In Missouri, 28 per cent of all those over twelve years of age were so classed. In Kansas, 42 per cent of those over twelve were classed as nonchurchgoers, and in liberalized Maine, 65 per cent. (These findings were published in 1916 in the *American Journal of Sociology*.) Studies such as these, and the frequent change of scene which they involved, helped to ease the shock of Alice's decision, and carried me through a very trying period.

At Christmas, in 1911, Alice did consent to correspond again, and in the letter in which she gave that consent she said that she was interested in me and all that concerned me. These words are graven in my heart. Again, I did not, perhaps, take full advantage of the opportunity, in that my letters were not as full or as frequent as they might have been. Nevertheless, in the spring, when I announced my intention of taking a church, she wrote a rather long letter in which she spoke of her skill in keeping house and making doughnuts. I took this as my opening and I replied accordingly. To this she responded in a stinging letter, saying that she had never loved me and that her answer had been given and could not be changed. I was stunned by her letter. Once more I gave way to the reaction of weakness and despair, and in my reply I spoke of the promise on which I had counted. Following this, the privilege of corresponding was withdrawn. My memory is hazy, but I think she said something about having been "weak."

Meanwhile, Fred Eastman had accepted a pastorate in Locust Valley, Long Island, where he was to do an outstanding job, and I, hoping still that Alice might relent, went as Congregational college pastor to Iowa State College at Ames. It was a challenging task. I was to live at the College, getting acquainted with students and faculty and using the resources of the College in the service of a nearby country church. But I went there in a state of mind little favorable to successful work. My usefulness was over by the end of the first year.

In the early summer of 1913, my grandmother passed away in the old home in Indiana at the age of one hundred and one. In her later years she was alert and active, but her sight, hearing, and memory were badly impaired. Her care, which had fallen on my mother, was no easy task. Grandma had been accustomed to running the household, and she did not readily surrender her authority.

I returned to Bloomington for the funeral services and stayed on a couple of months to help in the disposition of the old home. Since the house had been in possession of our family for fifty-four years—eighty, if we include the tenure of Andrew Wylie, my grandfather's cousin, and the first president of the University, who had built the house—that task was both difficult and interesting. My grandfather's library we turned over to the University as evidence of the kind of scholarship for which the University stood in the days when it was young. This library included not only scientific books of the period and a classical library but also some valuable incunabula and other ancient books which had come from his father's library. Among these was a fine copy of Ortelius' *Orbis Terrarum* and a Holbein Bible. The University was much interested in this library, even though it had been seriously raided, but most of all it was interested in our attic, where we found a number of important documents relating to the history of the University and of the state.

Toward the end of the summer my sister, who immediately after graduation in 1900 had married Morton Bradley, a promising young Indiana alumnus, at this time head of the fiscal department of the Boston and Maine Railroad, returned to her home in Arlington, Massachusetts, taking Mother with her.

I went, with sobering thoughts, to my new assignment in Wabaunsee, Kansas. This charge was a small country church, paying a salary of six hundred dollars a year and providing a parsonage. But again the task was a challenging one. The "Beecher Bible and Rifle Church," as it was called, had been built in 1857 by a company of Abolitionists from New Haven, men who had come west to help Kansas free itself of the institution of slavery, and had received, each one, a Bible and a Sharpe's rifle from Henry Ward Beecher and his church. My church had thus a fine tradition and it was located twelve miles from Manhattan, the site of the Kansas State College of Agriculture. We hoped, with the help of the College and of the Manhattan Congregational Church's pastor, Arthur Holt and his associate, Willis Goldsmith, to make it a sort of experiment station in rural church work. It was much the same idea as that at Ames, but here I was to center my attention upon the church and its constituency. My task was to inaugurate a vigorous country-church program. All sorts of community projects were undertaken. With contributed labor we built half a mile of sidewalk from the railroad station to the town hall and the two churches. We organized an athletic club and a singing society. We promoted play festivals. We arranged an excellent lecture course. We made a survey of the tuberculosis situation in the community and got the State Commissioner of Public Health to come from Topeka and discuss it. We made another survey of the wheat, corn, and livestock produced in the community. On the basis of this survey the chief of the College's extension service met with us and presented a plan for organizing a co-operative grain elevator and store. We also arranged a number of "farm demonstrations." With some farmer as host who specialized in thoroughbred cattle, a specialist in animal husbandry from the College would be present to discuss the fine points of that specialty. Or some farmer who had an orchard of which he was proud would invite his friends and neighbors over to meet a specialist in horticulture who would discuss the special problems of the orchardist.

It was somewhat the same general pattern I had followed in the Adirondacks. I was "up to my neck" in all sorts of activities. I was urging my people on before they were ready to go, and I met with difficulties. The first difficulty was with the community's other church. To that church I was a threat. Its members were not enthusiastic in their support of our "neighborhood association" and of its community-service projects. Then my own people began to balk. I left after two years, feeling that all was a failure, but taking with me one thing of crucial importance in the years that have followed, the friendship of Arthur Holt.

In view of this second failure, I was now being advised by my friends to go back into social studies. But I still felt that my main contribution ought to be in the field of definitely religious work, and I could not give up the hope of redeeming myself in Alice's eyes. Therefore, I took a church once more, this time in North Anson, Maine, at a salary of nine hundred dollars a year. Here I stayed two years. I had by this time learned some lessons. I was better able to listen and to wait, but I was still centering my attention upon programs of community service. I think I can say that in this pastorate I was not a failure. The church held its own, and I was not thrown out. But there was no great growth.

There was no change in the situation so far as Alice was concerned. After leaving Lowell early in 1912, she "rested" while working half-time in Cleveland. Then in 1913 she took a position with the Young Women's Christian Association on Chicago's West Side. I tried unsuccessfully to see her during my stay in Wabaunsee and again while in North Anson. One gain there was. Since 1912 there had been no recurrence of that physical reaction of weakness. But I felt myself to be in the situation of a man who has ventured to climb some great mountain, and finds himself in mid-air, unable to get any foothold or any refuge. To find some validation of the faith which had led me, I was ready to grasp at anything. The very fact that Alice refused me any satisfaction left me, I felt, with no alternative but to strive to become in some measure worthy of her. Never once did I entertain the thought of giving up.

Then came World War I.

I at once applied for a position as secretary with the Overseas Young Men's Christian Association and I was among the first to be sent to France, arriving there in September, 1917. I was immediately assigned to the machine-gun battalion of the First Division's Sixteenth Infantry. Though I did not know it at the time, I was with the same regiment which my mother's grandfather Richard Dennis had commanded in the War of 1812. In May, 1918, I was transferred to the Forty-Second, or "Rainbow" Division. Here I met with an artillery regiment from my own home state of Indiana. They were shooting over my head all the time we were in the Baccarat sector of France. When we left for the Champagne defensive, the boys from Indiana University asked to have me assigned to their battery. Throughout the rest of the war I traveled with Battery F of the 150th Field Artillery, seeing action at Château-Thierry, St. Mihiel, and the Argonne, and marching with them to the Rhine. Norman Nash, the regimental chaplain, later bishop of the Episcopal Diocese of Massachusetts, to whom I am so deeply indebted, was my associate during the twelve months I spent with this Division.

When the Forty-Second left for home, I went with my old chief, Warren Wilson of the Presbyterian Board of Home Missions, to start a school for our soldiers not far from Coblenz. Dr. Wilson, who had come to Germany under the auspices of the Young Men's Christian Association on an educational assignment, had conceived the idea of helping the boys to understand and interpret, with minimum reliance upon textbooks, the experiences with which they were being confronted. In accordance with that idea he himself undertook a sociological survey of the village of Grenzhausen, where we were billeted. I had a class in history in which, under the guidance of an elderly German forester, we began by visiting the old Roman front-line trenches, the "limes," which resembled so strikingly the trenches with which our boys were familiar. We inspected the old Roman watchtowers, which had been reconstructed by the University of Bonn. We visited a castle on the Rhine and examined the coats of mail there on display, and from this castle we gazed at the factories and cities of industrial Germany. Our guide piloted us also through the communal forest. After each of these trips we met and discussed what we had seen, and considered its meaning. After some ten days of fascinating exploration, I was "called on the carpet." It had come to the attention of the commanding general, Johnson Hagood, that I was teaching the boys German forestry. He wanted it clearly understood that I could teach all the French forestry I wanted to, but no German forestry!

Upon my return to America in July, 1919, I found a job

awaiting me. American churchmen at that time were dreaming great dreams. The world was to be made safe for democracy. President Wilson's hope was to become reality. To that end they had organized the Interchurch World Movement, and as a first step a world-wide survey was to be made. I was offered the position of director of the North Dakota Rural Survey.

But first of all I had a problem of my own which needed to be solved now or never. All through the war the thought of Alice had been with me. Even though we had not written to each other I had kept track of her. I knew that she was still in Chicago but that in 1918, because of the long and irregular working hours, she had left the Young Women's Christian Association and was working in a bank. A trip to Chicago was therefore imperative. This I took, but I found her adamant in her refusal to see me. I was dazed. It seemed an impossible ending. But I did not give way to the reaction of weakness, as in the earlier rebuffs. For several days I remained in Chicago, pleading with her. Then there came upon me a trancelike state similar to the one in Washington in 1908, and with many of the same ideas. It seemed that there must be some other man and that I was standing in the way. I wrote then, telling her of that Washington experience and of my readiness to make any sacrifice for her sake which it represented, even to the point of giving her to another man. Her reply to that letter was silence.

Back in Buzzard's Bay, Massachusetts, at my sister's summer cottage, I felt that I was going to pieces. I therefore wrote declining the position with the Interchurch World Movement which had been offered me. Shortly after I had mailed this letter, it came to me that this was a weak and unmanly thing to do. I therefore wired my acceptance and went at once to Fargo, North Dakota.

Then it came to me that I had been incredibly blind and stupid in my dealings with Alice, and on my arrival in North Dakota, I began to write to her regularly, giving much time and thought to the letters and trying to make them interesting and helpful to us both. To this plan she gave her consent. Accordingly I wrote a long account of my experiences with the Army overseas. I worked out an illustrated lecture on the country church. I wrote out several sermons, and I tried to formulate anew a confession of faith. These productions, as I read them over now, still seem worth while. They should have helped to allay the fears for my sanity which she may have had. In any case, she wrote several times briefly; and in a longer letter which I still have, she explained her position, her willingness always that we should be friends, provided it were clearly understood that it was and could be nothing more. I replied that I had rather have just her friendship than the love of any other woman in the world.

Meanwhile, things had not been going well with the Interchurch World Movement, and it had become clear that the Movement was going to fold up. At this juncture I received a tempting offer from Arthur Holt, whom I had known at Wabaunsee. He was now director of the Congregational Social Service Commission and he wanted me to join his staff, with a study of the Congregational colleges of the country as our first project. After careful consideration I decided against it. I still felt that my chief contribution ought to lie somehow or other in working out the message which seemed to me implicit in the religious experience through which I had passed, rather than in the gathering of facts and figures on social and religious conditions. More than that, I was counting now on Alice's help.

My hopes ran high when in June of 1920 she invited me to

call on the way back east from North Dakota. In her letter she said that she was still uncertain about the wisdom of her decision to see me. However, she wrote, if I would not be daunted by the presence of three maiden ladies and would not expect her to make an opportunity for me to talk with her alone, she would be glad to have me come to dinner with her "family." This family, she explained, included her sister Anne, and their friend, Miss Catherine Wilson, who was like another sister. Of course I was not "daunted." Sharp at six-thirty on Sunday evening I was admitted into their five-room apartment some five miles out on Chicago's West Side. And so we met for the first time in nine years. I found her all that I had dreamed, with only the changes a man would wish to see in the woman he loved.

She did not permit me to see her again and she was still emphatic in saying that her first answer was final and could not be changed; but of this visit she wrote that "something really tangible had been accomplished," and she expressed her pleasure that I had decided to take a church.

IV

A LITTLE-KNOWN
COUNTRY

INTO THE DEPTHS

MY PLANS for a pastorate ran into unexpected difficulties. Churches were not too plentiful, especially for a man whose record as a pastor had been no better than mine. Wherever I was being considered, the first question was likely to be, "Are you married?" and the second, "Do you expect to be married?" Neither of these questions could be answered in the affirmative. I would then be told that I must be content with a "modest" church. This meant, I soon discovered, a salary so low as scarcely to permit marriage if things worked out as I still hoped they might. It seemed as though I had come up against an impassable wall.

I was therefore forced to wait. I found temporary employment at the Interchurch offices in New York, and Fred Eastman invited me to visit him at his home in East Williston, Long Island. Fred, by this time, was well started on a successful career. His Locust Valley pastorate had been a very happy one. During the war he had done his bit as business manager of the *Red Cross Magazine,* and he had just taken an important position as educational secretary of the Presbyterian Board of Home Missions. He had married Lilla Morse, one of our former class-mates at Union. With them and with their two boys I spent a delightful six weeks. Each evening we took a short automobile ride, spent an hour and a half at work, played a few hands of "500," and turned in usually by ten o'clock. I was in the best of physical condition, and the future was looking really hopeful.

Early in October, 1920, I returned to the home of my sister in Arlington, Massachusetts, where she and her husband had just purchased a twelve-room house quite close to the Center. Here they lived with their two children, a girl of fourteen and a boy of eight. Mother made her home with them. Here I at once started to do something which I had been turning over in my mind for a number of days.

Nine years before, when Fred Eastman and I had come up together before the Brooklyn Presbytery, we had been required to write out and submit a Statement of Religious Experience and a Statement of Belief. It seemed to me that I was now entering upon a new period and was in a very real sense offering myself anew. Would it not therefore be fitting that I should try to reformulate my message and re-examine my religious experience?

On October 2 I began work on the Statement of Religious Experience, writing it in the form of a letter to my old pastor, Dr. Luccock, who was at that time chairman of the committee on vacancies of the Presbyterian Church. It covered in about four thousand words what is now included in the preceding portion of this record. I then turned to the Statement of Belief.

I threw myself into the task, became intensely absorbed in it, so much so that I lay awake at night letting ideas take shape of themselves. This was for me nothing new. Writing has never been easy for me, and it is only under strong feeling and concentrated attention that ideas begin to come. I was therefore merely following what I regarded as a necessary and, for me, normal method of work. This time, however, the absorption went beyond the ordinary. I was no longer interested in anything else, and I spent all the time possible in my room, writing.

All went well for three or four days. I completed the Statement of Experience and began on the Statement of Belief. While working one day on the Statement of Belief—I think it was Wednesday, October 6—some strange ideas came surging into my mind, ideas of doom, ideas of my own unsuspected importance. With them began the frank psychosis, as shown in the documents which follow.

Here is the Statement of Belief as I wrote it:

I believe in the Love which came to my rescue on that Easter morning long years ago, the Love that has pitied my weakness and borne with my failures and forgiven my sins, which has lighted my way through the dark nights of despair and has guided me through the awful wilderness of the insane, where the going is difficult and very dangerous. I believe that this Love is one with the God who through all the ages has sought to make himself known to the children of men.

I believe that this God was once perfectly revealed in the life and teaching of Jesus of Nazareth. His patience with our shortcomings, his compassion upon our infirmities, his unfaltering faith in men, even in his enemies, and his method of dealing with them, not through force, but through the power of love, culminating in his death upon the cross, where he died, the just for the unjust, the perfect for the imperfect, the strong for the weak.

And this process has been going on for nineteen centuries. The strong have been giving themselves for the weak and the perfect for the imperfect. A crossing process has thus resulted. The divine, in consequence, has been coming into the world disguised in ugliness, crippled by disease, shackled by sin, and impotent with weakness.

I believe that the weak and the imperfect should no longer accept this sacrifice and that they should be willing to give their lives, the imperfect for the perfect and the weak for the strong, that the divine may be freed from its prison house of infirmity and be able to come into the world in beauty and in power and not in disguise, and that the reign of love may be able to replace that of brute force and ruthless competition, where survival goes to the strong and to the merciless. And even as the divine has pitied our weakness and loved us in our imperfection, so the weak and the imperfect should take pity upon its suffering and impotence.

I believe in the immortality of the human soul and in the survival of the personality. I believe that life consists of two cycles, one in the flesh and one in the embryonic condition. These cycles consist of strong-weak and perfect-imperfect combinations, in which the strong is mated with the weak and the perfect with the imperfect. I believe that a reversal of this combination would secure a better race. This would come through the refusal of the weak and the imperfect to accept their claim of pity and of need. I believe that such a refusal will alone release the divine from its prison-house and enable it to overcome the world. This should do away with death and establish communication throughout the world.

I believe that the family should consist of four and not of two, of the strong and the perfect and of the guardian angels, who in the joy of serving and sharing in the happiness of those they love will find compensation for the sacrifices which some will always have to make. And the guardian angels, no longer in the darkness of the tomb, but in the light of life, may select for those they love the true mate and the true friend.

I believe that the Kingdom of God will be a new order of society, founded upon the principle of love and governed by the Great Spirit who wills that not even the least of his little ones should perish, but that all should have life. All shall then live together in harmony with each other and with the laws of the Universe, and poverty and pain and disease shall be done away. And there shall be no more death, for the cycle will be completed, proceeding from generation to generation and from one world to another.

Within this Statement of Belief it is possible to observe the transition into the abnormal state. It began without evidence of undue exaltation beyond what may have been implicit in the plan itself, but about the end of the second paragraph a change occurs. I can remember distinctly [1] how it came to me as I was sitting at my desk there in my sister's home on October 6, 1920, trying to determine what to say and pondering over what I had included in my ordination statement of nine years before. Suddenly there came surging into my mind with tremendous power this idea about the voluntary sacrifice of the weak for the sake of the strong. Along with this came a curious scheme which I copied down mechanically and kept repeating over and over again, as if learning a lesson. This scheme is shown in the diagram on page 82. Where it came from I cannot imagine. I can remember nothing in my previous reading which would even remotely suggest it. It was indeed precisely this fact which

[1] As of 1923, when I was copying the letters given me by Dr. Worcester and trying to record what I could remember of the experience I had been through (see p. 144). In that effort I had the benefit of memories which were still vivid. I had also before me the Statement of Experience written at the time of onset (see p. 78). This in turn drew upon the Statement of Experience written in 1911 for presentation at the Brooklyn Presbytery, and this again in turn drew upon a record, now lost, which went back to Washington in 1908 and to the Easter experience of 1898. The continuity of these experiences may probably be assumed.

so impressed me. Besides, the impact was terrific, and I felt myself caught up, as it were, into another world.

S Strong	P Perfect
W Weak	I Imperfect

There were other ideas, those of "life in two cycles," of an "embryonic condition," of "guardian angels," all coming from no known source, but receiving little or no further attention. But the idea about the voluntary sacrifice of the weak for the sake of the strong and of the family-of-four remained constant, not only in this but in subsequent episodes. It seemed to have meaning. It seemed that there were other men in the same position as myself. Their only hope of salvation lay in their love for some good woman, and in that fact lay hardship and suffering for the woman, and a real loss to society, since it would be only the finer type of woman who would be moved by such an appeal. There ought to be a way out, and the family-of-four scheme seemed to provide the answer. The essence of this idea was that of producing a thoroughbred type of character by setting the best types free from the appeal of those whose love was based on need. This was to be done by letting them choose mates, each for the other. Just how this was to be done was by no means clear, beyond the one principle that the true lover must be willing to give his place to another and that all self-seeking must be ruled out.

This Statement of Belief therefore demanded of me that I should give up the hope that had dominated my life for seventeen long years. Everything then began to whirl. It seemed that the world was coming to an end. This planet which we call the Earth was just a tiny organism in the vast universe, and now after millions and millions of years of development, a period long only to us, it was hurrying on at a rapidly accelerating speed toward some impending change. It had become mature and a transformation was about to take place. It was like a seed or an egg which had stored up within it the food materials which the new being will need, and the new being, as it develops, draws upon the reserve of food until it is used up. Then it breaks through the outer covering and emerges into a new environment. So now after all these millions of years humanity was just beginning to draw upon the stored up resources, and already after the short space of a hundred years, some of those resources are approaching exhaustion. Some sort of change was due. Only a few of the tiny atoms we call "men" were to be saved. I was not to be one of these. I might, however, be of help to others.

Momentous issues were therefore involved, and I sent the two documents to Fred Eastman, together with a letter elaborating upon the ideas contained in the Statement of Belief, particularly that of the family-of-four. The high tension under which this letter was written is evidenced by the fact that the typing is almost illegible, due to an improperly adjusted ribbon which I was too excited to fix. This letter was written immediately after the Statement of Belief. It reads as follows:

DEAR FRED:

Nine years ago you followed one of your class-mates to Missouri. You found him a crotchety fellow, hard to get along with, and you had to part with him. But you forgave him. You helped him when he was out of work. You have taken him into your home and fed him. You have helped him in innumerable ways. Such things you have been doing right along. You have eyes to see where need exists, and a heart to respond. I look upon you as my best friend, a perfect friend, and I come to you with a problem which concerns me deeply.

I have been having some strange ideas these last two weeks. You may think that I am insane, for the problems with which I have been concerned lie beyond the usual. But some of them may be important.

May there not be something to this idea that our present system of mating is one of competition and that every time a child is born another possible child has to give up its right to exist. The "family of four" plan, by doing away with the cross-breeding, could prevent such loss and bring into the world not the spiritual averages, but the positives and negatives. If it is true—and it seems to me reasonable —that life consists of two cycles with a strong-weak and a perfect-imperfect combination, then a double positive in the one makes a double negative in the other. Thus my father would be a strong-strong-imperfect, while I would be a weak-weak-imperfect. And we both have to perish because no one will recognize him in "one of these least." The very strong can only be produced by permitting the very weak to exist. The man whose love is really nothing but a despairing call for help has little chance of finding that help in our present system of mating.

It is my deep conviction that my case is not one of

ordinary insanity. I have not been bothered recently with troublesome thoughts, and the motive which has sustained me throughout this affair is not desire but the conviction that I was really acting in obedience to a divine command. I thought that command was to go forward, but it seems not. It is rather to get out of the way. If it is really true, as it has come to me, that I represent a personality which for nineteen centuries has been trying without success to solve one problem, then I have been an impediment in the fight, and it is time for me to give up. Victory, after all, is only won at the cost of sacrifice, and the right response to the sacrifice on Calvary is voluntary self-sacrifice on the part of the unfit. The sacrificial acts of the old Testament were inflicted upon the victims. The sacrifices we will now be called upon to make will be self-inflicted and in accordance with the law of love. . . .

And yet I feel that there has been some definite purpose in this journey of mine. That purpose, it seems, is to give my place to some other man. I want a chance for my father and for what he could do in the world. The one woman who has the power to make this possible will think me insane if I write to her directly. You offered once to make a trip for me, if it should be necessary. I should like to have you go and see her and lay the case before her. You have been a perfect friend. Therefore I dare to ask this of you. My thought would be a quiet ceremony, a little time together. Then I would eliminate myself. I could not ask such a thing for myself, but only for my father.

If the matings of the future are in fours, then it should be easy to produce and maintain the great man and his opposite.

This letter was not included in the record which I gave to Alice in 1923. Immediately after mailing it to Fred Eastman I was greatly horrified by it, and in the letter I sent her I reverted to the idea that there must be some other man.

It will be clear that I was becoming more and more excited and bewildered, and the ideas were more and more foreign to my usual modes of thought.

For several days I said nothing to my family, but finally I broke the rule of silence and began to share my fears. Then came another source of terror. After talking somewhat freely one morning, it came to me that there were other forces, hostile forces of which I had not dreamed before. There were, it seemed, other dimensions of which we are not ordinarily aware. It seemed that the world was all ears, and the words which I had spoken would bring about my undoing, and defeat the cause with which I was concerned.

On Saturday afternoon about three o'clock, according to a letter to Fred Eastman of November, 1920, I suddenly felt a sickening sensation, something I could not account for. I went down at once to see Mother and told her that something awful had happened. I did not know what it was, but I thought I had been "betrayed." Then I went into the next room and found there a man I did not know. This was a physician who had been called in, but I did not know it at the time, for he did not question me. He just watched and listened.

Meanwhile, my family had become greatly alarmed and I was myself not without some appreciation of the situation. I recall[2] remarking at supper on the final evening that the problem of insanity was of great importance, and I had determined to investigate it. But my first intimation that they were thinking of sending me to a hospital was when six policemen came marching into the room where I was working, and one of them announced that I had better come quietly or there would be trouble.

The size of the squad gave evidence of my family's alarm.

[2] A memory as of 1923.

I have, however, not only my own memory but their assurance that there was at no time any manifestation of violence on my part.

The story of the week that followed I wrote two and a half years later for Dr. Macfie Campbell's seminar at the Boston Psychopathic Hospital, the institution to which I was sent. It reads as follows:

I was brought to the Psychopathic Hospital on Saturday night, October 9, 1920, about 10 P.M. and stayed there until the following Saturday or Sunday. I was then transferred to the Westboro State Hospital. The length of my stay was thus about one week, but it seemed like thousands of years. Throughout this entire period I was in a violent delirium and spent most of the time reposing in cold-packs or locked up in one of the small rooms on Ward 2, often pounding on the door and singing. How much of the time I was unconscious, I do not know, but I can remember quite distinctly what was going on in my head as well as my actual behavior. It has seemed to me worth while to make a record of these memories while they are still relatively fresh in my mind and yet far enough away so that I can see them in some degree of perspective.

My first memory is that of Dr. Gale filling out the admission blank, and of one particular remark he made. I had asked that I might be taken to a certain friend whom I trusted, because I did not want to talk to doctors whom I did not know. Dr. Gale said, "That is clear proof that he belongs here."

Just what happened that night I do not remember. Perhaps the knock-out drops had begun to take effect. The next thing I can remember happened the next morning. I was lying on the bed, apparently asleep, when I heard one of the nurses say, "He is here on a homicidal and suicidal charge. There must be some mistake. He does not look in the least violent. He ought to be on Ward 4." This hit me like a thunderbolt. I knew that I had never had the slightest thought of injuring any one, and as for the idea of taking my own life, that had been held only for a short time and immediately rejected. Such a charge was clear evidence that evil forces were at work.

That morning I was transferred to Ward 4. Here I was subjected to a lot of personal questions by a nice-looking young fellow who did not have on a white coat. I was introduced to another patient who was said to be a Harvard professor. His name, I believe, was Nicholls. But I kept getting more and more excited. I was invited to play checkers and started to do so, but I could not go on. I was too much absorbed in my own thoughts, particularly those regarding the approaching end of the world and those responsible for the use of force and for the charge of homicidal intent. By nightfall my head was all in a whirl. It seemed to be the Day of Judgment and all humanity came streaming in from four different directions as in the accompanying diagram. They all came in to a common

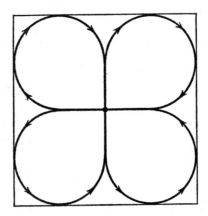

center. There they were brought before the judgment seat. But it seemed to be an automatic sort of judgment. Each individual judged himself. There were certain pass-words and they made certain choices. Each person had three chances: a difficult "right the first time affair," a second choice which involved an element of sacrifice and meant that one would become a woman and not a man. The other was only a seeming chance which sent one at once to the lower regions. These lower regions did not seem to be anything very fixed. The whole thing was like a vast circulatory system. Each human being was like a corpuscle in the blood stream and we all kept going around and around and around and around. All the time choices were being made and some were being sent below and some above. I had at the time the idea that my consciousness had gone to a lower level. Something, I thought, was short-circuited.

That night, as I lay in bed, the idea came surging into my head: "You are in the wrong place here in this comfortable ward. You ought to be down-stairs." I thereupon requested that I be allowed to go to the other ward. The attendant replied, "Go back to bed or we will have to take you to Ward 2." Seeing that nothing was to be gained by requests, I took his suggestion and began to raise a disturbance, calling out at the top of my lungs the first and craziest thing that came into my head. This happened to be, "I've got to go insane in order to get married." I was thereupon promptly removed.

In Ward 2 I was given first the little room in the south east corner. I was tremendously excited. In some way, I could not tell how, I felt myself joined onto some super-human source of strength. The idea came, "Your friends are coming to help you." I seemed to feel new life pulsing all through me. And it seemed that a lot of new worlds were forming. There was music everywhere and rhythm and beauty. But the plans were always thwarted. I heard what seemed to be a choir of angels. I thought it the most beautiful music I had ever heard. Two of the airs I kept repeating over and over until the delirium ended. One of them I can remember imperfectly even now. This choir of angels kept hovering around the hospital and shortly afterward I heard something about a little lamb being born upstairs in the room just above mine. This excited me greatly and next morning I made some inquiries about that little lamb. One of the other patients, whose name I believe was Gardner, drawled out, "Say, stranger, did you ask about a lamb? There was one left in my room last night." This, of course confirmed me in my belief, and I immediately accepted this fellow-patient as the embodiment of a very exalted personage, who as I thought had assumed this form and with it a very loathsome disease of some sort. I tried to talk with him to find out something definite. There were, it seemed, certain tokens left by the angels which were to be exchanged between us. But no sooner did we get a few words together than the attendants would be upon us. Before long I found myself locked in my room. But Gardner, who was still free wandered up and down the ward whistling and smiling. I thought there was some sort of system to it which I could not quite catch, and it seemed to me that he soon had the whole ward happy. The ceiling seemed to be raised and the entire room resonant with music. But I was worrying about that lamb, and I kept inquiring about it. The idea came, "The doctors were very much interested in it and they immediately killed it and preserved it in alcohol because of its scientific interest."

During the day I was visited by a certain Dr. Klopp, who was said to be a distinguished physician from another state. He had heard that I had some important ideas about saving people. He was very much interested in this problem and he wondered if I would be willing to tell him about them. I rather liked Dr. Klopp's looks, but I replied that I had rather not talk. He immediately went away. This raised my opinion of him greatly and made me think I had made a mistake. Several times afterward I inquired about Dr. Klopp.

The next night I was visited, not by angels, but by a lot of witches. I had the room next to the one I had occupied the night before. There was, as I remember it, nothing in it but a mattress on the floor. It seemed that the walls were of peculiar construction. There was, it seemed a double wall and I could hear a constant tap-tapping along the walls, all done according to some system. This was due, it seemed, to the detectives in the employ of the evil powers who were out to locate the exact place where I was. Then the room was filled with the odor of brim-stone. I was told that witches were around and from the ventilator shaft I picked up paper black cats and broom-sticks and poke bonnets. I was greatly exercised, and I stuffed my blanket into the ventilator shaft. I finally not only worked out a way of checking the invasion of the black cats, but I found some sort of process of regeneration which could be used to save other people. I had, it seemed, broken an opening in the wall which separated medicine and religion. I was told to feel on the back of my neck and I would find there a sign of my new mission. I thereupon examined and found a shuttle-like affair about three-fourths of an inch long.

In the morning Dr. O'Brien wanted to know why I had put that blanket in the ventilator shaft. I thought there was an evil gleam in his eye, as he spoke. Then I made some remark about the sign on my neck. The doctor laughed a peculiar laugh and said he'd better put some iodine on it. He started to do this but I broke away and ordered him to be careful. He seemed to be frightened, though I had no thought of touching him.

I believe that the examination before the staff came on that day, Tuesday, October 12, though I am by no means sure. As I remember it, there were a number of women present, who sat, most of them, on the south side of the room. I think it was in the library rather than in the assembly-room on the third floor. I cannot remember the books, but I do not recall climbing any stairs, and I remember very distinctly that when the examination was over, I took it into my head to wander down the corridor, to the east and was promptly subdued by four or five attendants.

As to the examination itself, I can remember Dr. Campbell's pleasant manner and his snapping eyes and the many questions he asked me. Most of the time my answers were very slow. I was sunk in my own thoughts and I tried to wait until the answers came of themselves. The questions seemed to center about my ideas of the "family of four." Other questions had to do with my delusions of grandeur. I had myself something to say about having come to the end of the trail and having gone all the way around the circuit. I also expressed my indignation at being brought in before all those women in a bath-robe. I was also indignant at being brought to the hospital by force. I could not talk unless I were free. Dr. Campbell made some remarks about the need of avoiding force in committing patients. This raised my opinion of him but it did not mollify me sufficiently to permit me to shake hands with him when it came time to leave.

Then followed my first, though not my last experience in a cold-pack. I was much interested in the proceedings and saw two possible explanations. Dr. Campbell had just extracted from me the admission that I was a very exalted personage. Either they were going to exploit me in some horrible way, or else there was a more benevolent purpose, that of demonstrating to me the error of my ideas of grandeur. As nearly as I can remember, I really hoped that they might succeed in the latter purpose—for those ideas were agonizing—and I awaited the results of the demonstration with much interest. But all that happened was that I became unconscious. That for me was the usual effect of the cold-pack. Aside from these periods in the cold-pack I did little sleeping.

The following night I seemed to be in some labyrinthine tunnels deep down in the recesses of the earth. Part of the time I was drugged with what I was told was "bismuth." This, it seemed, was the drug they used to preserve the old Egyptian mummies. It was a very peculiar drug, and the amount of it one had in his system determined to what level he belonged. There were thirty-two such levels. At the thirty-second level a man would be utterly prostrate and unable to rise except as some one should come and give him pure water to drink. At one time I was thus prostrate.

A little later I found myself wandering through these subterranean tunnels until at last way down deep I came upon a horse-blanket within which was wrapped up some peculiar white linen fabric. These it seemed were some most sacred relics. They were connected with the search for the Holy Grail and represented the profoundest spiritual struggle of the centuries. Then I found that by lying flat on the floor near the ventilator shaft, I could hear the most beautiful voice I had ever heard. It was the celebration of the Last Supper. Towards morning it came to me that I must begin with the single cell and that I must make friends with a certain attendant for whom I felt a particular dislike. I tried to do this and I thought he seemed very well pleased with himself. A little later he brought me my food, an unusually generous portion, but I refused to eat it, because I thought it was drugged. I remember also some voices going through a ritualistic service in a sing-song fashion which was distasteful to me and sounded insincere. They kept repeating over and over again the phrase, "Little lamb, little lamb." I thought I recognized in the priest the attendant with whom I had tried to make the alliance.

I had now come to the place where I no longer distinguished day from night. I had become an old stallion who had remained behind at the time of the flood in order to help his friends escape and had been forgotten by them. He was now imprisoned and exploited by a lot of un-principled medical men and nurses. The only way of escaping was by having my head cut off. I was locked in my room now and I kept getting wilder and wilder, singing and shouting and pounding the glass on the door with fists and elbows. I was ordered to be quiet but this only made me pound the more violently, until I was placed in a cold-pack once more.

Then I found myself in the Moon. The idea of being in the Moon had been present almost from the beginning of the week. Now this became an outstanding feature. The Moon seemed ordinarily quite far away, but really it was very near. The medical men knew about it and they had perfected a way of spiriting people away and burying them alive in a cell in the Moon, while in the meantime some designing person, a sort of double, would take their place in this world. Everything was run in a very strange way in the Moon. It was done in the most scientific manner. It seemed that it was the abode of departed spirits and all the interests were frankly and openly concerned with the problem of reproduction and of sex. Really it was quite appalling. It seemed that upon one's advent in the Moon the sex was likely to change and one of the first things the doctors tried to determine was whether you were a man or woman. They had certain delicate instruments for determining that. When they examined me I heard them say in great surprise, "He is a perfect neutral." It seemed that the needle was not deflected in either direction. I was thus not consignable to either side and thus they had no power over me. In that lay my hope of safety, also in the injunction, "Tell the exact truth," instead of depending upon some token or pass-word as others did. It was very important to be on one's guard, for it seemed that they had a peculiar custom of chopping off one's head and sending one down an invisible chute to the lower regions. This was done in a matter of fact, scientific manner, just as they slaughter cattle in Chicago.

At one time I succeeded in climbing into the sun, but through some clumsiness, I managed to destroy the balance of things and my friends and relatives in the sun suffered heavily in consequence. Thousands and thousands of them lost their lives. Their blood seemed to gush into my throat and I was nearly strangled with it. I kept groaning, "My friends, my friends, my friends." But I kept struggling in the effort to restore the balance and keep the floor of my room from tipping up and sending everything down to the lower regions.

I was engaged in this interesting occupation when the door opened and several men appeared, among them Dr. O'Brien. They had my clothing with them and they wanted me to put it on. It was of course part of a plot to undo me, so I refused and resisted. I had therefore the honor of being transported to Westboro in a strait jacket.

PERIOD OF REMISSION

The transfer to Westboro State Hospital took place about October 16, 1920. For about two weeks I remained acutely disturbed. Then I snapped out of it, much as one awakens out of a bad dream. Early in November, I was transferred to the convalescent ward, and I began at once trying to figure out what had happened to me. I tried to recall and record all that I could. I studied other patients and I besieged doctors and nurses with questions. What happened at Westboro is best told through the letters I wrote at the time.

The following letter was written about three days after my transfer from the disturbed ward, and the day after I had been assigned to the convalescent ward. The visit referred to was on

Thursday, November 4, and the letter was addressed to the friend with whom I had been staying on Long Island.

November 8, 1920

Rev. Fred Eastman
East Williston, L.I.
DEAR FRED:

I wish to express my deep appreciation of your taking the time and trouble to look me up. Your visit has meant a lot to me. It has been for me as though I were dead and am alive again. I am feeling much stronger and really quite like myself.

I am grateful for the spirit with which you have taken this thing. As I look back upon it, I find much that makes me blush and shudder. And yet I still feel that the story of these last twenty years is not wholly a mistake. I believe that there is in it a deeper meaning. In spite of the violence of the disturbance, I have not felt myself deserted. I have come through feeling that there has been no break in the purpose of all these years.

What the future may bring forth remains to be seen, but I feel hopeful. Only one thing gives me apprehension—the prolongation of my stay in the hospital. I do hope I may soon be restored to normal conditions among my friends.

The second letter to Fred was also written in November of the same year. If my memory serves me correctly, I began it on Thanksgiving Day and finished it the following Sunday. It was received at East Williston on December 4. It was thus written within a month from the time I emerged from the psychotic condition. It was my response to a letter from Fred suggesting that I should make mental illness my special problem.

DEAR FRED:

I have been doing some thinking along the lines of your suggestion, and since I now have plenty of time on my hands, I am going to set down some of my provisional conclusions.

I suppose every inmate of such a place as this has ideas and theories of his own and feels much aggrieved because others will not accept them. I feel, however, that I have some understanding of my own case. I have been dealing with it for twenty years, and you will remember that practically all my Seminary work centered around this problem.[3] What I shall give you is therefore really the result of twenty years of study, rather than just recently formed conclusions, except in so far as my conclusions have been influenced by this recent experience.

As I look around me here and then try to analyze my own case, I would distinguish two main types of insanity. In the one there is some organic trouble, a defect in the brain or a disorder in the nervous system, or some disease of the blood. In the other there is no organic difficulty. The body is strong and the brain is in good working order. The difficulty lies in the disorganization of the patient's world. Something has upset the foundations upon which his ordinary reasoning processes are based. Death or disappointment compel a re-organization of his world from the bottom up. That, I think, has been my trouble, and it is the trouble with many others also.

You have, if I remember aright, a fairly full account which I gave you last month.[4] I may therefore point out that the key is to be found in the Easter experience of 1898. A new idea brought relief and hope and newness of life, when all had seemed darkness and despair, an idea

[3] The reference here is to my interest in the psychology of religion and of mysticism. At the time this letter was written I did not know that such a man as Sigmund Freud existed. My work in the psychology of religion had been done under the guidance of Professor George A. Coe, who held that his job as a specialist in the psychology of religion had nothing to do with the pathological.

[4] The reference here is to the Statement of Religious Experience in the letter to Dr. Luccock, which is embodied in enlarged form in Chapters II and III of this record.

so tremendous that it necessitated a reconstruction of my entire philosophy of life. . . .[5]

Now my diagnosis is this: What is involved in my case, as well as in many others, is a sort of autohypnosis. I recall that in one of Professor Coe's seminars at Union we discussed the various means of inducing the hypnotic condition. The principle brought out was that the key to it lay in the narrowing of attention to a single object or idea. One of the group went home and proceeded to fix his attention upon an electric light bulb. He succeeded, but he also injured his eyes. I take it that my attention was concentrated so completely upon one idea that hypnosis in some form was just what might have been expected. Of one thing I am sure. There was nothing wrong with the mental processes or with the reasoning faculties. Once my premises were granted, the conclusions were at least understandable. The fundamental fallacy was, of course, the assumption that an idea carried authority because of the way in which it came.

I have been especially puzzled regarding the origin and significance of the ideas of grandeur. How is it possible that I could ever fancy myself in such exalted roles as I did in the insane period? I see two possible explanations:

1. When you give everything you have for a certain end and you then feel yourself called upon to give that thing up, it is equivalent to giving up your life; and your life is for you one with the world and with the universe. This principle is expressed mathematically—if my memory does not betray me—by the equation $1/0 = \infty$. It makes no difference how small or insignificant the unit may be, if it is divided by zero the quotient is infinity.

[5] Here follows a lengthy and poorly written paragraph in which I point out that all my major decisions have been made automatically and they seem to have worked out well, even though some of them have been made under a deep sense of personal failure. In the present instance, 1920, there seems to have been progress, rather than failure. For eleven years there had been none of these automatic decisions, and this time I had approached the crisis feeling that I had done my part.

2. When you give up, or think you are giving up all that makes life worthwhile, you don't care about anything else. Wealth, power, honor have no particular charm. You don't care about them, and you know that you don't. You therefore feel no enormity in the ideas of grandeur, much as you may later be horrified by them. They are felt rather as a burden which is wholly unwanted.

Concerning the particular ideas I shall not attempt any explanation. I would only insist that periods of crisis are fertile in suggestions, some of which may stand the test of experience and some may not.

I would stress the fact that most of these ideas were not in line with my previous experience and thinking. In fact they derived their authority in my thinking precisely from the fact that they were so absolutely different from anything I had thought of or heard of before, and because they came surging into my mind with such a rush.

A few days after your visit I was called to the door. Dr. Chambers, the assistant superintendent, was there. With him were two men, and he wanted to know if I recognized them. They were the men who had brought me out from the Psychopathic. After a short talk Dr. Chambers remarked, "Quite a change, isn't there? It's certainly a good ad for the hospital." Of course, I was glad to hear him say that. I am indeed appreciative of all they have done for me here, but with his conclusion I cannot agree. If I have recovered, as I think I have, I cannot ascribe it to the methods of treatment, but rather to the curative forces of the religion which was largely responsible for the disturbed condition.[6]

At Westboro I was also violent, but there was no solitary confinement there. I was either in the tubs or else on a large sleeping porch with a score of other patients. I got a favor-

[6] At this point in the letter comes an account of the period of onset which is quoted on p. 86. This is followed by an account of the week at the Psychopathic Hospital which is given in greater detail in the paper for Dr. Campbell's seminar on pp. 87 ff.

able impression of the doctor, but I was still suspicious of the nurse and of the chief attendant. I thought the food was doped. Here also I thought I was engaged in the same great struggle and here also it seemed that the Christ spirit was embodied in one of the patients, a young ex-sergeant whom I saw helping other patients who could not help themselves.

One of the things which excited me very much was the treatment given in the hydrotherapeutic baths. I looked upon it as a sort of punishment or persecution. I would go repeatedly to the door of the tub-room and ask to take the place of one of the men whom I regarded as among my friends. One day—I think it was October 27—when I went there with this request I was ordered to stop. When I did not immediately obey, three young attendants threw me down on the floor and began to beat me up, starting in the small of the back and working upwards. I was then carried back to bed. After staying there a little while, it came to me that I had done wrong in going back so easily, that I ought to have made them finish me up and that only thus could I release the spirit I thought imprisoned within myself. I went back then and was given a more severe beating. I can feel the effects of it now, even after five weeks. One of the older attendants told me later that I was given what was known as "the old bughouse knock-out." As I was being carried back—for I was not able to walk—I had the momentary consciousness of being once more myself. For a day or two I was not able to get up. Then on October 29, which happened to be my birth-day, I seemed to wake up. On that day I was brought before the staff and my doctor remarked, as I was leaving, that I had done pretty well.

One thing which all during my stay in the disturbed ward had much to do with the persistence of my delusions was the appearance of the Moon. I saw it centered in a cross of light. I took that as proof that I was right in ascribing great importance to what was happening to me. The cross stands for suffering. Therefore the Moon knows and the Moon is suffering on my account. But on Wednesday night, as I lay awake on the sleeping porch speculating on this dire portent, I made a discovery. When I changed my position to a certain spot, the cross no longer appeared. The explanation was simple. From that particular spot I was looking at the Moon through a hole in the wire screening! That discovery was a big help toward recovery. The next day I wrote a letter to my sister for the first time. In the afternoon came the visit from you and from her. These visits definitely repaired the broken communications and did so the more effectively because they came on that particular day. After that I improved rapidly and within a week I was transferred to the convalescent ward. This change of ward released me from many hold-over suggestions which had power over me so long as I remained on the disturbed ward.

This is a long and wearisome and fragmentary account of a very unpleasant experience. I have given it with a definite purpose. It suggests what seems to me a very important principle: *The cure has lain in the faithful carrying through of the delusion itself*. It also shows that the treatment given only made me more violent. So far as I can recall, I have never refused to do anything when I was requested to do it by some one in whom I had confidence. Nevertheless, I have been given severe beatings, all because in my bewilderment I did not obey some harsh order by some young attendant. There was little attempt to make use of persuasion or to cultivate hopefulness and self-respect.

The fundamental difficulty seems to me this: A man whose fundamental derangement is not of the body but in his philosophy of life is sent to a place where they look only at the physical side. Most of the doctors, I think, are not religious men. Many of them regard religion as a superstition which is responsible for many of the ills they have to treat. Such men are not fitted to deal with religious problems. If they succeed in their aims, the patient is shorn of the faith in which lies his hope of cure.

As for myself, I have from the beginning recognized the abnormal character of my own experience. I have recognized that those experiences which have been for me so vitally important would be classed by physicians as insanity. But I have chosen deliberately to follow the thing out. I have been following a trail which has taken me through some very dangerous country. But I believe it has been worth while, and I would make the same choice again. Even this experience, painful though it is, may be an adventure of which use can be made. There has been in my experience so much of the pathological that it is perhaps a fitting end to my life's adventure that it should lead me to an institution such as this and should open my eyes to an important task which needs to be done. The only wonder is that I escaped hospitalization in Washington, where it would probably have been fatal.

Sunday

I have just been talking with Dr. D., a charming young doctor whom I like very much. He tells me that I can go home Christmas, if my family will invite me, and he encourages me to believe that by New Year's, or shortly thereafter, I can be released entirely. I was, however, disappointed to have him leave me with the suggestion that my great mistake has been in not giving freer rein to the sex impulse.

In reading over this document, one or two things make me pause. Have I, perhaps, failed to recognize sufficiently the need of force in such cases as mine? That need I take for granted. I do not suppose that I would ever have gone to the hospital willingly. My grievance is rather the lack of any attempt to use persuasion or to explain what is being done and why.

The other point is my apparent failure to recognize the

seriousness of this disturbance. My answer is that there is hardly any need of stressing the gravity of my situation. The hopeful factors are less apparent, and it is upon these that any constructive future must be built. I do feel that I have made a long journey through some difficult and little-known country and that I have come through intact.

The following letter was written shortly after receiving a copy of Freud's *Introductory Lectures* from Fred. This was my first introduction to Freud, and I became very excited over finding in this book much that supported my independently-arrived-at ideas.

December 11, 1920

DEAR FRED:

Let me thank you heartily for your fine letter and for the book on psychoanalysis. I have been reading it with intense interest and, in fact, excitement. Freud's conclusions are so strikingly in line with those which I had already formed that it makes me believe in myself a little bit once more. I refer in particular to two propositions:

He asserts in the first place that neuroses—i.e., abnormal, or insane conditions—have a *purpose*. They are due to deep-seated conflict between great subconscious forces and the *cure is to be found not in the suppression of the symptoms but in the solution of the conflict*. That is just what I tried to say in my last letter.

The other proposition is that concerning treatment. He recognizes three stages in the process of cure:

1. There must be absolute frankness and truthfulness on the part of the patient, understanding of the trouble on the part of the physician, and the attempt to bring into clear consciousness the dimly understood ideas which should prevail.

2. He holds that in practically every case of successful treatment in which the sex instinct is involved, the patient's

affections are transferred to the physician. This, he says, is a fact that must be frankly recognized and wisely utilized as fundamental to the process of cure.

3. Re-direction or sublimation or elimination of the transference as soon as the right time comes. This marks the completion of the process of cure.

As I understand my own case, that is precisely what has been happening. Therein lies the explanation of the recent smash-up. May it not be the destruction or sublimation of the transference relationship and the completion of a process which has been going on for many years?[7] That, at least, is the interpretation I had arrived at before I ever heard of Freud. I am glad to receive support of this sort. It makes me feel as in the days of old when I was working on some difficult problem in algebra, and then after getting my answer, I would turn to the key in the back of the book and find that my answer was right. But this is a problem on which I have been working for eighteen years.

My idea of the "family of four" would then be an attempt to express this principle. The idea I had in mind would be this, that there are those for whom the hope of salvation is involved with sexual love. This fact must be recognized. This does not mean, however, that such a desire should be gratified. If it is the right kind of love, it would not demand that. On the other hand, it must not be killed. The surgeon's knife and the methods of fear and repression are not the right treatment, but frankness and co-operation. It seemed to me then that the finest men and the finest women are precisely the ones most likely to respond to the appeal of weakness and of need. Such a response has had blessing attached to it, but it has also meant sacrifice which should not have to be made. Of course, in my abnormal condition I went too far and at-

[7] I remember clearly what I meant here. The "physician" in my case would be Alice. See p. 55.

tempted to universalize my own experience, but may there not be some element of truth in this crazy idea?

I remember distinctly the beginning of that idea. It came first during that abnormal period in Washington,[8] a flashing, blinding, overwhelming idea that I was not after all just what I had thought myself, but that I had lived on this earth many hundreds of years under different forms but always with the same problem which I had not been able to solve. It seemed that I was identified with the woman from whom the seven devils had been cast out; also with the poet Dante. Confirmation of this I found in the fact that my first illumination had come on Easter morning, that the problem was indeed the same, and that the idea was one I had never dreamed of before. It seemed also that in that struggle lay the center of the fight which had been going on for nineteen hundred years. The Christ personality had been imprisoned and crippled by the selfish demands of a love which had been essential to some weaker person's salvation. He had been imprisoned because he could not destroy the weaker personality in his own interest; also because this problem, that of sex, represented the first and most difficult problem in the making of a better race. It seemed that as a representative of that weaker type, it was my duty to give up what I felt to be my claim. After I had acted on that it seemed that the fight had been won, and I became ecstatically happy. Then I was seized with a terrible panic from which I emerged only gradually.

One of the things which has most puzzled and horrified me in this recent delirium is the ideas which I have had regarding my own identity. Starting with the idea that I was the representative of the Magdalene-Dante type, I surrendered my claim and became a zero quantity. Then

[8] Cf. p. 59. This somewhat fuller account was written while at Westboro without any documentary aids. It may include ideas which were distinctive of the episode of 1920.

I became confused. I was a zero quantity, but I was also its opposite. Another idea which persisted throughout the disturbed period was that I was a representative of the sex instinct. It was in this role, I think, that I attempted repeatedly to eliminate myself. Once I tried to drown myself in the tub and nearly succeeded. Twice I rammed my head against the corner of the brick wall.

As I look back over this, viewing it more in perspective, I still wonder if there may not be some glimmering of truth in these strange ideas. We know so little about the unseen forces. Is it not possible that our minds are the scene of a struggle in which universal issues are at stake?

One such idea was that of life as consisting of two cycles, one in the flesh and one in the spirit. It seemed that the departed spirit had its abode in the subconscious of those whom it loved and that its chances of returning to the world and perpetuating the cycle depended upon the fidelity of the man or woman in whom that spirit abode. According to this idea, it should be possible, if we learned the laws, to select the types which are brought into the world and thus secure an unbroken succession of alternating personalities. That would be eternal life. I am giving this just the way the idea came.

The universe I thought of as a great living organism, or series of organisms. It seemed that out of the present world a new social order was to be formed. This would be a new spiritual body gathering to itself the spirits of those who were fit. In such a body the "family of four" would constitute a new type of cell replacing the simpler cell on which the present order is founded. It seemed that the present order is based upon competition, and competition eliminates the best as well as the worst. The new order would be based upon co-operation and would seek to preserve whatever was worth preserving, guarding carefully the finest and the best. According to this idea, the virgin birth of Christ would represent an actual new element entering into the race and it was made possible by some man giving his place to another. But the Second Coming had not taken place because of the frailty of some of the disciples. It seems that the personality which I represented had been chiefly responsible for blocking the way. Salvation was thus by no means assured. It depended upon the outcome of a titanic struggle which was still undecided.

During the disturbed period I had over and over again ideas of going through all stages of evolution from the single cell on. It was all very terrible.

My sister says I talked of dying in order that I might be born into the world again. I cannot remember any such idea as that.

I am setting this down just as accurately as I can as part of the analysis I am trying to work out. I hope you will keep this together with my other letter. I have no place to file things here and I may want to refer to them again. I feel like a traveler back from a distant country and I want to record my observations while they are still fresh. This does not mean that I hold to these ideas as true. While I do believe there may be some truth in some of the ideas, I am concerned chiefly with the mental processes which are involved.

I am much interested in your suggestion regarding transfer to the Bloomingdale Hospital [in White Plains, New York]. If they use the Freudian method there I should like to go there in order to watch the results. I am well enough contented here. I am treated well. But I want a chance to study other methods of treatment than those prevailing here.

As I wrote you last time, my doctors says I can go home Christmas if the family invites me and that I can be released shortly after New Year's.

From the middle of December until early in March of 1921, the correspondence was concerned chiefly with the obstacles to an early release and with negotiations for transfer to the Bloomingdale Hospital. My letters during this period indicate a fair degree of stability. There was however a brief period in mid-December when some of the old fears were threatening to return. This is reflected in the following letter dated December 16, 1920.

DEAR FRED:

My sister tells me that you have been much upset by the thought that all these queer ideas of mine were evolved under your own roof. Let me assure you that such was not the case, at least so far as the abnormal state was concerned. I had never thought of such things before nor had I read of them. They were just ideas which came to me suddenly and insistently as from an unknown source and I simply wrote them down.

I do hope you may be able to make some arrangements by which I can get out soon. I should prefer not to be transferred to another hospital but to come out under your care. Frankly the thought of having to bare my very soul again is by no means pleasant to me. One of the hold-over ideas I can't get away from is fear of the doctors and fear of imprisonment.

This morning a bunch of us were sent out to get laurel for Christmas decorations and I was ordered to show the way to an especially good place which I had visited in company with our kind-hearted, nature-loving head-waiter. It filled me with fear and forebodings. I can't bear the thought of taking a crowd like that out to strip the bushes of leaves and flowers, so that all their beauty will be destroyed for the coming year, if not for several years to come. I fear something of this sort for myself. I don't like to be dissected as a pathological subject. I don't want to say more than is necessary and then only to those I trust absolutely.

About the middle of December, while talking with one of my physicians, I remarked that while I recognized the grotesque character of the ideas I had had during the disturbed period, I still felt that in the experience there had been some purpose. It was not all a mistake. He shook his head solemnly and said I was entirely wrong. This remark of mine apparently cost me the visit to New York upon which I had been counting. In any case it explains the following letter to Fred Eastman under the date of December 30, 1920.

DEAR SIR:

Replying to your letter of recent date, I beg to inform you that I do not consider Mr. Boisen well enough to visit you at your home during the coming week-end. He still has many false ideas and although his conduct is not greatly disturbed, it is easy to see that his mind is far from right. He still believes that the experience through which he has been passing is part of a plan which has been laid out for him and that he has not suffered from any mental illness. This mistaken idea is sufficient to tell us that he is still in need of hospital treatment.

Very truly yours,
W. E. LANG
Superintendent

The reference to my believing that I had not suffered from any mental illness refers, of course, to my attempt to distinguish between cerebral disease and mental disorder, and my assertion that I had no cerebral disease.

In fairness to the doctor it should be said that in talking with him, talking as I did under unfavorable conditions and vexed by his attitude, I probably got somewhat excited. It was this which probably explained his answer.

The chief developments during the month of January were

the completion, through Fred Eastman's unremitting efforts, of the negotiations for my transfer to the Bloomingdale Hospital in New York and my own growing conviction that my vocational future was to be found in the mental hospital. But the way was by no means easy, and when it came time to have the necessary papers signed, serious obstacles were encountered. It was a trying time for all of us, especially for my mother. My own state of mind is reflected in the following letter to her.

1 February 1921

My beloved Mother:

I have been pondering this morning over the next step which lies before me. I have already written you of what I have in mind, but I feel that there is a little more that needs to be said.

It is for one thing clear to me that I cannot go back into the pastorate. The prolonged stay here has already made that inadvisable. In this Fred Eastman agrees with me. In fact both of us arrived at this conclusion independently. It is inadvisable because it would be necessary to account for these four months, and questions would be raised in the minds of many people, even though I were far more competent than I have ever been before. It is also inadvisable to think further of the pastorate because, if this experience which I have passed through has any meaning, that meaning would point clearly in another direction.

Two courses then remain. I can go into survey work, or other work which I have done before. Such a step I should regard as a backward one and I should always feel myself a failure. The other course is to take as my problem the one with which I am now concerned. That seems to me the clear course. It would give meaning and unity to the experiences of the past and provide something for me to live for and work for. This is truly an interesting and important problem, one which is just beginning to be understood and one in which religion and medicine meet. In many of its forms, insanity, as I see it, is a religious rather than a medical problem, and any treatment which fails to recognize that fact can hardly be effective. But as yet the church has given little attention to this problem.

My chief reason for wanting to go to Bloomingdale was to make contact with what I am told is the foremost institution in the country now concerned with the problem of mental illness. I want their help in understanding my own problem. I also want to study their methods. I thought that by going there as a patient, I would be far more likely to get their help in finding openings in this field. It is still my feeling that this would have been the best way.

Please do not think I am unhappy or unwell. I may be stubborn, but I do feel that there is nothing to grieve over in this apparent catastrophe.

Dr. D. suggested the other day that I ought to try to forget these abnormal experiences. My reply is that I *cannot* forget and that I can see *no reason to disbelieve.* It has all been consistent. It is only that things are working out more literally than I had anticipated. It makes life a very stern and exacting affair. What would there be to live for if the foundations of my faith were swept away? Facts are of course to be accepted in so far as they can be determined, but on beyond the facts is the realm of faith and we must believe and act upon our beliefs if ever they are to be realized. I see no reason to believe that my faith has not been supported by the facts, not, at least, after allowance has been made for ever-present errors.

Yes, my darling Mother, I do believe in prayer. I believe that its chief function is not to help us attain what we want, but to find out what is wanted of us and to enable us to draw upon the sources of strength which will make it possible for us to accomplish our task, whatever it may be.

My prayer now is that in this critical period we may

receive guidance and strength to do whatever is right and best in the long run; and if I have made any mistakes in the past, I pray for forgiveness and for the chance to set myself right again.

All during this period I had not written to Alice; neither had I heard from her beyond a kindly reply to a letter that I had written to her just before the commitment, which must have told her at once what had happened. In that letter I outlined my idea of the family-of-four, which, when I came to myself, seemed horrifying. My silence was due partly to the life-and-death struggle in which I was engaged, partly also to the feeling that letters written at this time would seem like appeals for sympathy. There was no lack of thought of her. It just seemed better to wait until the situation cleared.

The following letter of February 14, 1921, to my old comrade-in-arms, Norman Nash, then teaching at the Episcopal School in Cambridge, Massachusetts, offers additional evidence of the growing interest in the mental hospital as my future field of work. It reveals also an excessively critical attitude.

DEAR NORMAN:

Your inquiry as to my present whereabouts is not easy to answer. You will readily understand this when I tell you that I am at present an inmate of a hospital for the insane, where I was committed last October. As measured by the ability to work, to think straight and to maintain a fair degree of cheerfulness and confidence, I am now, so far as I can judge, as well as I ever was. But here I am, and no relief is in sight.

The cause of it all was an abnormal condition, similar to others I have had on four previous occasions. Each one of these has marked a turning-point in my life and, along with abnormal and pathological elements which I have always recognized, it has brought me what I have regarded as most sacred and most authoritative. This time I became bewildered and terrified until my sister in turn became frightened and I found myself committed. For three weeks I was in a violent delirium, which nearly proved fatal. Then on October 29, I seemed to wake up and in two more weeks I was as well as ever. But I am now in the hands of doctors who do not understand and with whose view-point I am quite at variance.

This catastrophe has of course destroyed my hopes and plans. I came back last July with the intention of taking a pastorate. From that I am now turned aside. My present purpose is to take as my problem the one with which I am here confronted. I believe that many forms of insanity are religious rather than medical problems and that they cannot be successfully treated until they are so recognized. The problem seems to me one of great importance not only because of the large number of sufferers involved, but also because of the religious and psychological and philosophical implications which inhere in it. I am sure that if I can make to it any contribution whatsoever, it will be worth the cost.

The hardest thing is to realize that those of us who are here are practically counted as among the dead. We have no standing in the eyes of the law. We have no rights. Our word counts for nothing, and our wishes, our feelings, our judgments are only so many reasons for doing otherwise. If I had to describe this place, I would say it is a place of weeping and gnashing of teeth, where the light is gone and the loved ones cut away, while those in control are industriously engaged in suppressing the symptoms which might lead to recovery, all too often through the agency of devils with the pitch-forks of authority in their hands. Over the door I would write, "Lasciate ogni speranza, voi ch'entrate." [All hope abandon, ye who enter here.]

Perhaps this is a bit strong, and yet I feel that it is not far from the truth. This is indeed a place of lost souls and the methods of treatment are nil. It is just a great prison which they call a "hospital."

I am not complaining of my present treatment. I am living very comfortably, too comfortably. I am accomplishing nothing. I am rusting, and sometimes I get very impatient.

RELAPSE

After three months of negotiations my mother and sister withdrew their objections, and arrangements were completed for my transfer to Bloomingdale, where I was to pay the nominal charge of ten dollars a week. The date was set for March 25, but on March 24 I became acutely disturbed and had to be sent to Codman Upper, a disturbed ward. The causes of this relapse were somewhat complex.

I had been eager to go to Bloomingdale; and yet, as the letter of December 16 shows, I dreaded the psychoanalytic treatment by men I did not know, perhaps even more than the incarceration at Westboro. For the psychoanalysts were doctors, and my fear of the doctors still carried over from my forcible hospitalization.

Then, back of it all was the conviction that I was not wholly wrong. I had been plunged into a strange new world, and the specific ideas from the previous delirium had been stowed away in the back of my mind with big question marks after them.

Just about a week before the transfer to Bloomingdale was to be made I was given a copy of *The Unseen Guest*.[9] This was a book on spiritism, one that does not make much impression upon me now, but at that time I became intensely interested in it, and under its influence the slumbering ideas were reawakened. They began to seem possible, then probable, then true. Meanwhile I had become more and more absorbed. I could

[9] Author anonymous (New York: Harper & Brothers, 1920).

think of nothing else. All night I lay awake thinking, all the time knowing that further detention at Westboro was sure to result. The dominant emotions were intense interest and intense fear.

My condition did not remain unnoticed, but the authorities were planning to go through with the transfer anyway. However, on the morning of the day I was to have left, I took matters into my own hands and visited one of the physicians in his apartment in order to discuss with him certain propositions pertaining to the family-of-four, which at that moment had become for me a plan of collaboration between medical and religious workers.

The following five letters to Fred Eastman show the development of my state of mind at the time of onset.

18 March 1921

DEAR FRED:

I had a talk with Dr. Lang this morning and learned with satisfaction that he had acted favorably to your proposition and that all that now remains to be done is to attend to the customary red tape. At first he was inclined to insist upon your coming to get me. Finally he consented to allow Mother to sign the needed papers and to let me go down to New York alone. I am hoping to be released next week so that I can be with you on Easter Sunday.

I have just finished *The Unseen Guest,* and have found it of absorbing interest. In fact the impression it made on me is tremendous. It seems to supplement and clarify and support so startlingly the experience through which I have passed and the ideas with which I have been struggling. Once more, just as in that book of Freud's, I have seemed to check up and find my answer right. I suppose I am pre-disposed to accept this book at face value. Perhaps for this very reason I ought to be more cautious.

20 March 1921

DEAR FRED:

The feeling is growing within me that before committing myself to the doctors at Bloomingdale I should like to talk things over with you carefully. You see, I have been doing quite a bit of thinking since I read the book you sent. It opens up a wide view and gives rise to questions which require intensive thinking. It draws my attention away from the problem of insanity to another problem of which I fear the doctors might not approve.

I am still planning to come down to New York Friday or Saturday night, arriving early in the morning.

21 March 1921

DEAR FRED:

I am very sad to-day.

Last November, after your visit here, you wrote me a fine letter in which you gave precisely the right suggestions. The time of my stay here is drawing to a close and the task you set me is unaccomplished. Your friend Anton Boisen has failed and his task remains undone.

My eyes are opened now through the book you sent me. I see and am much troubled. The failure is a tragic one. Its awfulness I can scarce imagine.

Have you noticed in reading *The Unseen Guest* that while the facts related there may be true, as I believe they are, it is not Christianity which it teaches. It implies a religion of ancestor worship. You notice, don't you, that Stephen is "of the same degree" and that the doctrine of evil and pain is inadequate. Evil and pain in this world are for him merely hallucinations. I tremble when I think of what this means.

I am feeling anxious about my release, for I am under a heavy strain and I am afraid they may keep me here, when what I need is to be with friends who understand. If anything should prevent my release this week, I fear for the results. The doctors have no understanding of my problem. I hope you will do all you can to hurry the thing through.

I see it all so clearly now. We are indeed just part of larger personalities, but with our eyes closed to that relationship. Our responsibility here is to do the allotted task. And I have failed.

22 March 1921

DEAR FRED:

In my recent letter I flew some signals of distress. I am sending you a few lines to-night to ask you to take those signals down. The problem has cleared up and all is right again. I suppose it is the fact of being still in custody which makes me so fearful.

I still feel that if I could get a place to stay and a little something to do outside of Bloomingdale, that might be a better plan.

I have not yet figured it out, but I am feeling rather happy now.

P.S. *One hour later.* It comes to me again that the situation is now very, very critical. Everything is hanging in the balance. I need your prayers and your help. You must get me out of here this week, no matter what happens. Oh, it is indeed terrible. Our Christian civilization is doomed and the battle will have to be fought all over again. It must now be fought against evil forces which are greatly augmented.

24 March 1921

DEAR FRED:

I am wondering if it will be possible for you to come to Boston Saturday night so as to be here for Easter. I am figuring on an experiment and I wish very much to have you here.

I am past my temporary feeling of fear now and I think I see the way. I shall not say more now. I will only add that I earnestly hope you will come. It may prove to be worth your while.

P.S. Let me add that I have figured out the cause of all insanity. The whole creation is organized in degrees. In each degree in thoroughbred stock is a family of four, corresponding to the type of family I proposed a while back. The line thus went in orderly connection, father-son-father-son, with the lines alternating. If for any reason this principle is changed, we have warfare. Like is unable to recognize like and we have ruthless competition. If in the Christian system of degrees the system is changed and the key family lost, then we have insanity. That link was broken at Calvary. Hence the turmoil and confusion of the last two thousand years, especially now, when during the World War the world has been violently insane. The great need now is to establish connection between God and the world, the connection which was lost two thousand years ago. I believe I have established that connection and I am asking you to come in order to see if I am right.

P.S. The connection was definitely established and passwords given and tokens exchanged. It was broken through the ruthlessness of the attendants.

These five letters have been given in full, notwithstanding their painful features, because they show so clearly how such disorders develop. We see in them the intense concern, the stepping up of the creative to the point of complete irrationality, and the abeyance of critical judgment. Ideas were accepted as authoritative because of the way they came, and the conscious self was down in the lower regions at the mercy of the strange and terrifying fantasms which flooded in upon it.

The attempt to understand and interpret this ideation in its particulars is most difficult. One thing only seems clear to me. The ideation in this second disturbance is similar to that of the first, and its meaning is to be found in the same struggle that was back of the first.

The disturbance that followed was quite as severe as that of the previous fall, and it lasted ten weeks instead of three. The following letter, also to Fred Eastman, was written during the third week of the disturbed period.

8 April 1921

DEAR FRED:

Just a few lines, while there is yet time, to tell you that I am still in the land of the living. I have, however, been deep down in the valley of shadow and I do not know whether I shall ever emerge.

Yes, I wrote despondently the week before Easter and I still adhere to what I said in those letters. The reality is far more terrible than I had ever believed and I fear the world is in for very troublous times. Christian civilization seems doomed.

I will ask you to ponder over that suggestion about the family of four as a means of keeping intact the family line. I think my suggestion that life is in two cycles is true and the family-of-four idea with unselfish love as the basic principle will be the means of preventing syphilitic infection and of breeding up the race until Christianity can come into its own.

I hope you will think of me kindly. My opinion of myself is not very high.

It may be noted that I was still dominated by the idea of impending world disaster and by the idea of the family-of-four. One reason for the persistence and strength of the latter may be found in the fact that the tubroom contained just four tubs. These stood in my mind for that idea. It seemed that it was a new type of cell, and it was associated with the idea of rebirth. It seemed that the psychopathic ward was the meeting place between this world and the world beyond, and the tubroom was the place for the regeneration of wornout personalities. I regarded it as my duty to stay on guard in the tubroom and I actually spent a large proportion of the ten weeks in that room. Somehow or other through those tubs the destiny of the world was going to be determined. It was my job to defeat the plans of those whom I regarded as enemies, some of whom, it seemed, were representatives of the devil himself. This required constant watchfulness, and throughout those ten weeks I scarcely dared to sleep.

All the time the idea persisted that if I could destroy myself, I could save the situation. On several occasions during the previous fall I had made such attempts. Now again I made repeated attempts. I had the idea that the way out was down and not up, and that I must descend to the lowest possible level. On several occasions I lay for hours during the night on the cold cement floor with no clothing on so that no one might be able to get below me and that the enemy might thereby be discomfited.

Symbolism was of course a prominent feature of such an experience. Things were not what they seemed to be. Everything had some deeper meaning. The patients around me were embodiments of good and bad spirits. So also were the attendants and the doctors. The different kinds of food all stood for something. I would eat no meat, no fruit, no pie, no sweet stuff of any sort, but lived on bread and water and beans, and very little of these. To have eaten of the other things would have brought misfortune upon my friends. But it was always a difficult matter to know what to eat and what not to eat. The different tubs also meant different things, though just what they meant I was not sure, and I was always wanting to be changed from one tub to another.

Gradually, however, some sort of solution seemed to be taking shape. The terror was disappearing and I was beginning to stay put instead of plunging around and throwing things into confusion. I was also getting fearfully tired and I was beginning to question some of my premises. But I kept going back to the tubs until I felt that nothing further could be accomplished. I finally consented to stay out if assured that I might be able to "help." I was then transferred downstairs.

Immediately then the old fears and the old ideas vanished, fears and ideas which, so long as I remained on the disturbed ward, were picked up from other patients or absorbed from old associations.

OPENING DOORS

I was transferred downstairs on June 4, 1921. The first week was spent doing little else but eating and sleeping and recuperating from the long ordeal upstairs. Then I began to look around for something to do. My first request for work met with the reply that I was not yet strong enough. This was the situation at the time of the following memorandum, which was written on June 15 and given to the physician the next day.

FROM: A. T. Boisen
To: Dr. Chambers
SUBJECT: Amusement on Codman Lower

It is now eleven days since I came to Codman Lower. During the first week I was chiefly engaged in recuperating from the ten weeks of tub treatment up-stairs and I did little but eat and sleep. This week, however, I am beginning to accumulate some surplus energy and I am looking around for some way of spending it to good advantage. To my surprise I find that this is no simple or easy problem.

The striking feature of this ward as compared with the other wards with which I am familiar is the *lightness of the ward work* and the *lack of occupation for most of the men during the major part of the day.* This results from the fact that there are no bed patients here, while more than half of the men are regarded as not yet fit for regular work. At this present moment (2 P.M.) twelve patients are at work outside the ward while thirteen are now here on the ward and have been here all day. These thirteen got up this morning between half past five and six o'clock, washed, dressed, took breakfast, and helped with the ward work. This was completed before nine o'clock. At ten we took half an hour's walk. The rest of the day we've been chiefly occupied in doing nothing. As I look around me here on the porch, I see one asleep, two are talking together, four are reading news-papers, five are looking into the dim distance and, judging by their expressions, they are thinking very gloomy thoughts. In fact, the remarkable thing is that more are not engaged in ruminating, for there is little else to do. There has been no work since nine o'clock, except in the kitchen and serving room, and there are no facilities for recreation. At present Codman Lower possesses the following recreational equipment:

    1 victrola—a treasure which is a great source of comfort to us all.

    1 set of checkers safely locked up in the reading room and accessible only by grace of the attendant.

    6 books, viz., Newcomb: *Popular Astronomy*, 1879
                Bruce: *Scientific Mental Healing*
                Roosevelt: *Hunting Trip in South Africa*
                Ralph Connor: *Patrol of the Sundance Trail*
                On Holy Ground
                Holy Bible

    Sundry copies of the *Saturday Evening Post, Ladies Home Journal, Country Gentleman, Harper's, Munsey's, National Geographic,* all much appreciated, but mostly consumed.

These books and magazines are now safely locked up in the reading room. In addition there are two books drawn by two men from the Patients' Library at Center.

My judgment is that some additional facilities for occupying the time and attention of the men on this ward would be beneficial. Speaking at least for myself, who generally have little difficulty in finding plenty to do, I would emphasize the fact that time does hang heavy on my hands and that the general atmosphere is one of gloom. I venture therefore the following suggestions:

1. The supplying of additional equipment for indoor recreation:

> 2 collapsible tables for cards, checkers, writing etc. (No tables at all are now available.)
> Sets of checkers, cards, dominoes, chess etc.
> Traveling library
> Bulletin board
> Book case
> 1 set of ring-toss

2. Equipment for out-door recreation
> Playground balls and bats
> Horse shoe outfit
> Volley ball and net

3. I would suggest further that more stress be laid on the daily walks. In addition to short walks on which all might go, there should be a longer walk in the afternoon for all the physically fit, and this walk should be made more interesting by varying the route. In this connection I would call attention to the fact that the walks are often omitted even when the weather is favorable.

4. It would seem to me advisable to have the reading room open more of the time. This is the more important because the dormitories are generally closed. I would suggest further that the older and feebler men, at least, should be allowed to lie down at times, especially after dinner. An opportunity to bathe before going to bed would also be appreciated.

5. Short talks on mental or personal hygiene by one of the physicians before the assembled patients might be helpful.

6. The fact that few of our men know about the Patients"

Library and that there is often difficulty in getting there during library hours should be noted.

16 June 1921

FROM: A. T. Boisen
TO: Dr. Chambers
CONCERNING: Work

In this morning's conversation the question of work was discussed and three possibilities were mentioned:

1. Checking in the laundry room
2. Work in the marking room
3. Photographic work (which might be occasional and irregular)

After thinking the matter over, I question seriously whether either of the first two would provide what I need just now. I am afraid they would offer little variety and would therefore prove irksome and confining. Of course I wish to be of service, but other things being equal I would prefer work in which I was interested and for which I had some aptitude.

It has occurred to me that it might be possible to combine the more or less irregular photographic work with an assignment to the wood-working department. This would mean work for which I have always had a particular fondness and of which I have done a good deal. I might, for instance, be given the job of making bean bag outfits or ring-toss sets for different wards, if this idea were approved, and I should greatly delight in making such things as bulletin boards and book cases.

16 June 1921

FROM: A. T. Boisen
TO: Dr. Dayton
CONCERNING: A Possible Fourth of July Program

In my work in a country parish it has fallen to me several times to provide for a Fourth of July program. I do not know the customs of this institution, but it has occurred to me that a play festival such as we have found suitable for our small communities might be in place here. I therefore suggest the following program for your consideration:

MORNING

9:30 to 10:30	Playground Ball	Talbot & Codman vs. the Rest
10:30 to 11:30	Clown-Rubes Baseball	Patients vs. Employees

AFTERNOON

1:30 to 2:30   Field Events
          Dashes—50 yards   Men: Fat Men
                        Lean Men
                        Free-for-all
                   Women: Fat Women
                        Lean Women
                        Free-for-all

Relay Races
   50 yard shuttle relay
   25 yard Sack race
   25 yard three-legged race
   50 yd. Wheel-barrow race

2:30 to 3:30

Special Features
   Pillow-fight
   Tug-of-War
   Nail-driving contest for Women
   Horse-shoe pitching

EVENING
Musical Program

These suggestions were approved. I was given the job of hospital photographer and I was authorized to go ahead with the Fourth of July program which I had proposed. This program went off with some measure of success and was followed by a more successful program on Labor Day, and then, during Christmas week, with a program of games for various wards.

Aside from the time needed to prepare for these programs, I filled my time with the photographic work. My task was to take pictures of the patients for the hospital records. This took me into all the wards, both male and female. I took between six and seven hundred pictures. I was also authorized to take pictures of the buildings and grounds and activities. This was of course a most agreeable task, for the attractive grounds and the varied architecture of the buildings called for whatever skill and artistic sense a photographer might have. In the course of this assignment I undertook to make a complete survey of the hospital in pictures. I also completed a rough topographic map of the grounds. All these things kept me delightfully occupied, and provided me with an unusual opportunity to study the hospital.

During this period I purposely avoided discussing my case with the doctors, even though my work brought me into close contact with them. More than that, I made no inquiries about getting out, beyond laboring with my friends outside.

The following two letters were written to Fred in the course of these negotiations.

31 July 1921

DEAR FRED:

I am sorry that I gave you the impression that my recent illness was in any way to be laid to your account because you had sent me a copy of *The Unseen Guest*. I remember

very distinctly that I asked you to send it. The responsibility was therefore mine. The last thing I would want
would be a censorship of my reading. Perhaps it is unfor-
tunate that I read it just at that time, but I am glad to have
seen it.

Your account of the labor situation is most discouraging.
Sometimes I think that if there is no work in sight it might
be a good plan to go back to the Seminary where I could
tackle this new problem with the help of such a man as
Professor Coe. It seems to me a problem in religion and
psychology and philosophy rather than in medicine. Such
a plan would have the advantage of giving me a new start.
I would not get that if I began as a scaler of logs or photographer or pastor of some little church.

I am bearing in mind constantly that in rejecting Dr.
Holt's splendid offer [see p. 75] in the survey field, my
feeling was that my chief contribution should lie in the experience through which I had passed. The recent catastrophe has not altered that view. It has only changed my
interpretation of my experience and has connected it up
with a very different field from that with which I would
otherwise have connected it. But the values in that experience still remain. I cannot for the life of me see that I am
any the worse for the recent disturbance. In fact, I really
believe there has been some progress. I hold with Prof. Coe
that the important consideration in any religious or mystical
experience is the result attained and not *how* it was attained.

I am glad to report that the celebration on the Fourth,
in spite of many short-comings from my point of view, was
regarded as quite a success. Apparently it was the first
thing of the sort attempted here. The photography is also
going well. This is the first time I have had a good dark room
with running water and plenty of chemicals. I have the
task of taking the pictures of all the new patients and I

am also taking pictures of the buildings and grounds and of the hospital activities. They granted me a few days ago the privilege of selling some of these views.

Dr. Chambers inquired this morning if I had heard anything from you recently. He then volunteered the suggestion that if I wanted to go to the Blomingdale Hospital, I could be transferred any time. That would, he said, apply to any form of release under sponsorship. My feeling is that if I have to stay in any institution of this sort, I had rather stay here where so much interesting work is opening up.

They are allowing me many privileges now. I went alone to Worcester the other day and my job as hospital photographer takes me freely into all the wards.

25 August 1921

DEAR FRED:

Your letter of August 20 is received. I have read it through carefully and I appreciate very much your frank presentation of the situation as it looks to you. Your letter reminds me of a remark you once made when President Wilson had just fired a man from the Cabinet. You said that letter was so beautifully written that you would be willing to be fired yourself just to receive such a letter.

From your standpoint, then, the situation in which I now find myself is anything but roseate. When analyzed, that situation is this: Periods of abnormality are likely to recur. They might recur while I was in the midst of an important piece of work or while you as custodian were away from home. You question, therefore, whether you could honestly assume the responsibility involved in such an office. You suggest, therefore, that I should accustom myself to the idea of remaining as an inmate here at Westboro. You feel that I could probably be more useful here, and therefore happier than I could be outside. But you say it all so beautifully and in such a genuinely friendly spirit that it is impossible for me to be hurt or offended. And, be-

sides, I am always glad to have the truth, for that consti-
tutes the only possible solution of any difficult problem.
I shall therefore try to answer the questions you raise, even
though in so doing I may go over ground already covered.

It would be foolish to deny the possibility of the recurrence of abnormality. Every such recurrence leaves its im-
press in the nervous system and makes it easier for another
one to recur. This must be frankly recognized, even though
I would dispute the physiological explanations held by
most psychiatrists. At the same time it is easy to exaggerate
the danger. In the seminar on mysticism which we had
with Professor Coe at Union he was constantly referring
to Delacroix's *Études d'Histoire et de Psychologie du Mys-
ticisme*.[10] It was, he said, by all odds the ablest study of the
psychology and history of mysticism which had yet been
made. This book I worked through very carefully, as you
may possibly remember. It was a careful analysis of the
experiences of Sainte Teresa, Madame Guyon and Heinrich
Suso, whom he had selected because of their recognized
standing and because of the sources of information available in their cases. As I remember it, he showed that in
each of these three there were alternating periods of exaltation and depression, the periods of exaltation being
marked by voices and visions and inspirations and automatisms of all kinds. Nonetheless they had an organizing
function. Their origin was to be found in inner conflict
and struggle. Their end was the unification of the personality. And as this end was attained the abnormal elements tended to disappear. But along with the constructive
experiences were elements which could not be assimilated.
These elements were rejected as suspicious, and taken
together they formed what he called the demonic current.

Delacroix seems thus in line with Freud in his functional explanation of insanity. He too finds the origin of
abnormal mental conditions in a conflict between certain

10 Paris: Felix Alcan, 1908.

subconscious forces, and he finds the remedy in the removal of the conflict. Where the conflict has to do with the sex drive, Freud would probably find the solution in a letting down of the bars and the removal of the inhibitions, at least to a certain extent.

I have tried to sum up these views of Delacroix because they fortify me in my own conviction that in my case the abnormal mental conditions are not to be regarded as chronic. If thirteen years ago I had been sent to a mental hospital, the doctors would have had reason to give me a gloomy prognosis. I was at that time in bad condition, morbid, bewildered, overwhelmed by a deep sense of failure. But now for eleven years there has been no recurrence, and this experience seems to me a problem-solving one. There has been throughout these years gradual progress in the direction of the unification of the personality—not in that of disintegration and degeneration. I do not believe there needs to be any recurrence.

How do I account for the recurrence of last Spring? . . . One factor was certainly the fear of this place and of others like it. While the dominating ideas were still much the same, the ideas most prominent in this last disturbance had to do with the imprisonment and the way of escape from it. There was the terrifying thought growing out of that experience that God himself was helpless in the hands of the doctors and that I must somehow or other help to set him free. It may also be noted that last fall when I came back to normal, it was largely the result of a severe beating which left me weak and helpless and unable to continue the struggle. In this disturbance on the other hand I fought my way through to some sort of solution. It was no accident that ten days after leaving the disturbed ward, I found the work in which I am now engaged. It was in line with the solution I had arrived at in Codman Upper.

I feel therefore that I am not ready to be junked yet.

But granting the danger of a recurrence, what should be done about it?

The answer will depend in the first place upon the character of the disturbance and the possible harm I might do to others. If I am a menace to society, I must of course be kept where I can do no harm. Thus far I find no evidence that there was even in the wildest delirium the slightest danger to any one else. I can remember most everything, and if given a chance I could give a very different interpretation to the words which were taken as indications of danger. In my own consciousness it was the best part of myself which was dominant throughout those disturbed periods and from the moral standpoint I was never more nearly right than at the very moment I was taken to the hospital. It was in some ways the highest point I had reached. That has been and is still my feeling. In saying this I am not forgetful of the shocking character of my ideas. I am thinking rather of my dominant concern with the grim problem of existence and survival, not of myself but rather of others. There was throughout no sexual excitation. And the ideas were fluid. There was in other words no Mr. Hyde personality, but rather a better self, blind and chained and struggling for release.

I recognize what you have in mind in speaking of the danger of a recurrence coming in the midst of an important piece of work. Last August you gave me a small job working up some statistics for your two books. Before that task was completed I went haywire, and the study was not completed in time to be of use to you. In general, however, the periods of abnormality have come in connection with some important transition or turning-point. They have not come while I was at work but in the "in-between times." And more than once I pulled myself together when in such a condition and have assumed responsible work and carried it through with some degree of success.

I appreciate your offer to help in any way you can. I do

not, however, think it will be necessary for you to act as custodian. I am hoping now that I may be able to take some work in the Harvard Divinity School and in the affiliated institutions which will help me to clear up the problems which this experience has brought to the fore and to prepare myself for a new task.

Perce[11] was here the other day and brought with him some good advice which he had hatched out coming down on the train. He urged me to take up concrete work of some sort. Such a course, he thought, would be the best means of helping me to regain and preserve my sanity. I replied to Perce that sanity in itself is not an end in life. The end of life is to solve important problems and to contribute in some way to human welfare, and if there is even a chance that such an end could best be accomplished by going through Hell for a while, no man worthy of the name would hesitate for an instant.

I often think of a little incident which occurred when I was in Washington. One of the old Forest School men had just returned from two years in the North Woods and a lot of his old class-mates were gathered around him while he dished out yarns about his experiences in the wilds. Finally one of the men asked, "Say, Bill, have you ever been lost?" Bill straightened up, glared at him, and replied with some heat: "Lost! Of course I've been. It's only the dubs who never go five miles from camp who don't get lost sometimes."

I agree with Bill. The kind of sanity which has to be preserved by sticking close to camp and washing dishes for the rest of my life is not worth preserving. I could never be happy or contented in such a course, especially when I feel that the particular territory in which I lost my way is of greatest interest and importance. I want to explore and map that territory.

[11] Percy Ladd, my roommate at Union, and a friend to whom I am deeply indebted.

There is one principle which seems to me very important. You are in doubt about a certain course. The facts are not known and cannot be known. In such a case the decision should be in favor of the course which promises the greatest returns, even though you cannot be sure you will succeed. I refer, of course, to the principle stated by Professor James in his *Will to Believe*. Of course I cannot be absolutely sure that there will not be a recurrence of trouble, but the possibility of such a recurrence should not in my judgment deter me from the course which promises the greatest opportunity for service.

In the course of my negotiations for release I wrote to my old teacher, George A. Coe, under whom I had done my major work at Union Seminary. I had hoped that as a specialist in the psychology of religion he might be able to help. The following letter, written in longhand, is one of many I have received from him. He followed closely all subsequent developments. Every reprint of an article of mine which I sent him was acknowledged with painstaking and illuminating criticisms. Although at this time he had no suggestions to offer, I still count him among the great teachers to whom I am most indebted. This letter reflects the attitude of many leading psychologists and theologians of that time, toward the problem of mental illness.

THOUSAND ISLANDS PARK, N.Y.
September 1, 1921

DEAR MR. BOISEN:

I have read your letter with keenest interest. It sounds just like you and I have difficulty in thinking of you as ever losing your poise.

If only I knew about mental disorders to diagnose them, I would gladly put my knowledge at your disposal. But I touch the subject at the outer fringes only, and then, very, very little. In fact, since you were at the Seminary I have been giving only diminishing attention to it, my energies being fully absorbed in the topics of religious education and the psychology of religion.

In general, too, my views of mental disorders, as far as I have views, tend in the physiological direction. I can see how mental habits can be formed, and I realize that habit is a large part of neurasthenia. But the question remains, Why just these habits in the neurasthenic and opposite habits in the normal person, the environment being practically the same.

If the attacks from which you have suffered are, as appears, rather severe, then your physicians are probably right in assuming a physiological root, even though the process whereby a given content arrives is that of suggestion. The fact that the specific physiological root has not been discovered hardly decreases the probability that there is one. I speak thus freely because you are so cool and objective yourself. I am glad that you have the disposition to face all the facts and that nothing needs to be concealed.

I sincerely hope that you will soon be a free man again. Meantime, how much you have to be thankful for, especially (in addition to skilled medical help) the interesting and important work of institutional photographer. I wonder whether you will go on to microphotography of diseased tissues.

This letter will bring you little of the help I would like to extend to you, but it is weighted with agreeable memories and hopes for the happiest outcome of your trouble. Please let me know after a while how it fares with you.

Cordially yours,

GEORGE A. COE

Since the exchange of letters with Norman Nash in February I had continued to keep in touch with him. He visited me two or three times in addition to writing, and during those visits we discussed the possibility of consulting Dr. Elwood Worcester of Emmanuel Church in Boston. We also considered the feasibility of my enrolling at Harvard for a study of the problem with which I was confronted. The following letters will indicate the progress of these discussions.

18 September 1921

DEAR NORMAN:

This is of course an anxious period with me. One by one the different means of escape on which I had been relying have been removed. . . . The plan [for doing graduate work at Harvard] in which you have been kind enough to interest yourself is now the only one remaining. But of all the plans which I have considered that plan seems to me to offer the greatest prospect of leading to something worth while. If it works out as I hope it may, I can even be thankful for the set-back of last spring.

.   .   .   .   .

I hold that there is no line of separation between valid religious experience and the abnormal mental states which the alienist calls "insanity." The distinguishing feature, as I see it, is not the presence or absence of the abnormal and erroneous, but the direction of the change which may be taking place. For the most part the cases with which the psychiatrist is concerned are cases in which the patient is losing ground. Valid religious experiences, on the other hand, are unifying. The subject is gaining ground, even though there may be much disturbance and many morbid and erroneous ideas. Saul of Tarsus, George Fox and others I might name are classed as religious geniuses, not as insane persons, because the experiences through which they passed had a constructive outcome.

It is worth noting that the procedure of the religious teacher has often been just the opposite to that of the present-day psychiatrist. The church has long taught that conviction of sin is the first step on the road to salvation. It seeks to make a man face the facts in his own life in the light of the teachings of Christ and to square his accounts, even though it may make him very uncomfortable. The psychiatrist, on the other hand, says, "Forget it." And very frequently he takes the position which one of our young doctors took in the only interview I have been granted since I have been here,[12] that the trouble has been in my idealism and that the thing to do is to let nature have its way.

I am unable to agree that further stay here is either necessary or wise. I am not unhappy. I am trying to forget myself in my work and I am fortunate enough to have plenty of interesting work to do. But I am well aware that so long as I remain here as a patient, I am by that very fact discredited. There is therefore little that I can contribute to the understanding of this problem. I would also be limited in my capacity to help others by the discouragement which might result from long-continued incarceration. It is also to be recognized that the longer I stay here the harder it will be to re-establish myself when I do get out.

You will, of course, not take anything I have said as a reflection upon my doctors. They have treated me most kindly and I am grateful to them. I am only trying to emphasize the difference in point of view which, as I see it, makes correct understanding in such cases as mine very difficult for them.

25 September 1921

DEAR NORMAN:

My mother was here Thursday and brought word of your call the day before. She has great confidence in you, and it was very heartening for me to see how much more

[12] During the preceding remission I probably pestered the doctors with requests for interviews and it is certainly true that they were not very responsive. Following my recovery, I purposely avoided discussing my case with the doctors, even though the work I was doing provided many opportunities to do so.

hopeful she is since your visit. She has still many lingering doubts. She wonders whether it would not be best to let me stay here until the doctors think me well enough to be turned loose without restrictions. She also has the idea, to me so abhorrent, that I must now engage in some sort of physical work. However, she is willing to be guided by whatever Dr. Worcester says and she will back me up in taking work at Harvard, in case he is favorable to that, even though the financial problem is going to be a difficult one.

Negotiations with Dr. Worcester were somewhat delayed because of his absence from Boston, but on his return he responded at once. There was then some difficulty in the matter of securing the needed information. This is indicated in the following letter.

WESTBORO STATE HOSPITAL
5 November 1921

Dr. Elwood Worcester
Emmanuel Church
Boston, Massachusetts

DEAR SIR:

Replying to your letter on November 2nd with attached letter from Mrs. Boisen, I wish to say that if you care to visit our patient, Anton T. Boisen at this hospital, I would be very glad to have you do so; or if you will designate a day and an hour when Mr. Boisen may call upon you in Boston, I will arrange to have him do so, provided of course that his mental condition remains as good as at the present time.

I might state that his case is one which is characterized by periods of acute excitement during which he is quite violent and attempts self-injury.

In accordance with the law, our records are not open for inspection.

Very truly yours,
W. E. LANG, *Supt.*

To supply Dr. Worcester with the information he wanted Fred Eastman forwarded to Norman Nash the letters I had written him. To these, Nash added my letters to him and turned them over to Dr. Worcester. My interviews with Dr. Worcester began, if I remember aright, early in November, 1921, and continued until May or June of the following year. I found them very helpful. We maintained communications until his death.

At the close of our conferences Dr. Worcester turned all these letters over to me, saying that I might sometime want to make use of them. The two following letters I wrote to Dr. Worcester during this period.

WESTBORO STATE HOSPITAL
20 November 1921

Dr. Elwood Worcester
Emmanuel Church
Boston, Mass.

DEAR DR. WORCESTER:

In the interview of last Monday the following ground was covered, if I remember correctly:

1. The precise nature of the original trouble.
2. The character of the first abnormal condition.
3. Some facts regarding the love affair around which the whole thing centers.
4. Your advice that I take up some outdoor work.

I hope that the following facts have been established:

1. The original trouble was primarily a mental one. There was no habit of masturbation and no perversions, as I understand those terms. There was difficulty in controlling the wayward sex interests.
2. The first abnormal condition, while containing many morbid elements, was a clear-cut conversion experience, with effects which were wholly beneficial.

3. The love affair was not rooted in friendly association but rather in inner struggle and in what might be called quite accurately the need of salvation. The motive power has been the deep feeling that this was for me the right course, the only one I could follow and be true to my best self.

4. The danger that I may underestimate the gravity of these abnormal conditions and the necessity of avoiding future recurrences. This danger I recognize. The horror of the recent catastrophe is with me still. It has been terrible beyond the power of words to express. And yet I do not regard these experiences as "break-downs." If I am right in believing that through them difficult problems have been solved for me and solved right, and if through them help and strength have come to me, am I not justified in such a view?

As I have tried to understand my own case and as I have studied the problems of others in this hospital, I have come to the conclusion that there are many patients whose problems are little different from those of many who go to hear Billy Sunday and "hit the saw-dust trail." They have no physical trouble. They are just sick of soul. Now to the physicians here anything in the nature of automatisms, any "voices," any visions, even a belief in providence or divine guidance is per se evidence of insanity and justifies commitment. Just last Christmas I was denied permission to visit a friend on the ground that I still believed that in the experience through which I had passed there might be the working out of a divine plan. And yet, as I understand it, some such faith has always been fundamental in the Christian philosophy of life. I think there can be little question that such men as Saul of Tarsus and George Fox would fare badly before a present-day psychiatric staff. Certainly they exhibited phenomena of abnormality. But with them the abnormality was a source of power and strength. I am therefore hoping for the day when cases of mental trouble which are not primarily organic in origin will be recognized and treated as spiritual problems and that the church will develop physicians of soul of a type whose work will be based upon sound and systematic study of spiritual pathology.

It is such a study that I desire to undertake and my desire to take work at some theological school is for the purpose of preparing for such a task.

In this purpose I am guided by my belief in the importance of this task, also by the faith that I can really make some contribution to it. It was the faith that my chief contribution should lie in the experience through which I had passed which led me a year ago last spring to refuse a tempting position with the Congregational Social Service Commission. I cannot see that the catastrophe of last fall should now destroy that faith. On the contrary, it seems to me to have widened the problem and to have thrown new light upon my particular experience.

EPISCOPAL THEOLOGICAL SCHOOL
CAMBRIDGE, MASS.
14 March 1922

DEAR DR. WORCESTER:

Your discussion—in the *Living Word*[13]—of the survival of the personality after death brings to my mind an idea which was very prominent in my thinking during the disturbed period. Much of that time I thought I was dead and that I was in some new and strange world. I did not know who I was. I was first one and then another personality, other and bigger than myself. There were thus delusions of grandeur so commonly found in mental disorder, and the recollection of them is painful. And yet I often wonder if there may not be an element of truth in these delusions.

May it not be that at death the individual consciousness, without losing the memories and associations which con-

13 By Elwood Worcester (New York: Moffatt, Yard & Co., 1913).

nect it with this existence and constitute the personality, passes into and merges with some larger personality? It would be much the same experience which a man has in moments of enthusiasm when he forgets himself in his devotion to some cause or some institution. It would be like the figure of the vine and the branches, in which the branch, supposing it had consciousness, would suddenly get its eyes open to the fact that it was not just a branch but was one with the vine. The center of consciousness would thus be shifted from the part to the whole.

If there should be in this anything of truth, then the greatest happiness which could come to any man would be to find himself one with the highest personality, which in my thought would be Christ. But many are those who have not made this possible. Some of these may have their part in him through identification with some lesser personality, some lower center of the organism. In other cases the interests may have been so selfish and perverse that the self-consciousness may find itself identified with some hostile personality, or it may gravitate toward some lower order.

At death, then, the group consciousness would supersede the individual consciousness, but the individual memories and associations would remain and through these there would be contact between friends who remain and those who have gone before. Such contacts might explain the providences, the sense of guidance which down through the centuries have figured so prominently in the lives of religious men. The Divine Spirit would thus be one and yet everywhere at once, taking thought even of the hairs of the head or the sparrow that falls. It would be analogous to the organization of the human body, in which the consciousness is of unity and yet not a cell can be destroyed or a nerve ganglion injured without having attention called to that fact.

I had also the idea that for each person there are two ultimate ends—eternal life and eternal sleep. Pain and suffering would thus be incidental to the process of growth and achievement. They would cease with the possibility of life and happiness. From this point of view they are ever to be welcomed and borne bravely. But for some the Hindu idea of escape from the evils of life may offer a blessed release.

During all this time the idea of some great Earth Spirit was present. The exact character of this spirit was not clear, but its high destiny lay in Christ. In him all our finest possibilities centered. But the world rejected him once and it has been continually rejecting him. For me during all that period the source of most of the torture was that it was now too late and that some overwhelming world catastrophe was imminent.

The disturbance is past now, but I keep wondering if there may not be some elements of truth in that idea. Certainly we are not justified in any great amount of optimism in view of the failure of the Christian nations to rise to the occasion when the greatest opportunity in history lay before them. In view of this feeling I have sometimes wondered if in the experience of the Hebrew prophets there may not have been a sort of madness in which the awareness of national danger was a determining factor.

This letter was written some seven weeks after I had left Westboro to take up my studies at Harvard. It raises a central question, one with which I had been faced in the experience which had sent me to the hospital. It is a question with which I have since been grappling in my efforts to discover the interrelationship between mental disorder and religious experience.

V

AN ADVENTURE IN
THEOLOGICAL EDUCATION

I LEFT WESTBORO toward the end of January, 1922, after a fifteen months' sojourn there, and took residence in the Episcopal Theological School in Cambridge, where my friend Norman Nash was teaching. With his help, arrangements were made by which I entered as a special student in the Andover Theological Seminary, which at that time was affiliated with the Harvard Divinity School. I was thus enabled to take a course in social ethics under Dr. Richard C. Cabot and one in abnormal psychology under Professor William McDougall. I was also admitted to Dr. Macfie Campbell's seminar on the psychology of belief at the Boston Psychopathic Hospital. In addition I took courses with Professor Henry J. Cadbury and with Professor Kirsopp Lake on the beginnings of Christianity, and I continued my conferences with Dr. Elwood Worcester at Emmanuel Church in Boston. Looking back, I often wonder where else I could have found a group of teachers so well suited to my particular needs.

Through Dr. Campbell I was at once introduced to the leading authorities in the field of psychiatry, and I was delighted to find that there was much support for the views which I had worked out independently. In addition to becoming better acquainted with Freud, I delved into Jung, Janet, and Adolph Meyer. I was particularly interested in Jung's theory of the "racial unconscious" and in his interpretation of human nature as purposive. Dr. Cabot was much interested in my story, and although he himself did not accept the psychogenic interpretation of mental disorder, he gave stanch support to my project.

As soon as possible I began looking around for a job. First of all I investigated the chaplaincy situation. I quickly discovered that the plan which I had found in operation at Westboro was the prevailing one. Most of our mental hospitals had religious services on Sunday, but they were conducted in the afternoon by ministers from nearby churches who knew nothing about the special problems of the patients. This arrangement was regarded as "good public relations," and there was no disposition to change. Any suggestion that a minister of religion had anything to learn or to contribute was coldly received. I even offered to serve as an attendant, but the stipulation that I should be given access to case records barred that out.

The summer of 1922 I spent chiefly in working up reports on Westboro, the first copies going always to Alice Batchelder, who on my release had granted me permission to write, in so far as it might be of help to me. I had spent seven months in making a survey of the hospital in pictures. I now organized these pictures and combined them with a study of the hospital and its operations, which I entitled "Studies in a Little-known Country." I spent much time editing and copying the letters which I had written to Fred Eastman and Norman Nash, and which they had given to Dr. Worcester and he, in turn, to me. A year later I brought these together under the title of "My Own Case

Record." It is this private, unpublished document which consti-
tutes the basis of the present book. And each week I wrote to
Alice according to the plan I had followed in North Dakota, trying to make the letters worthwhile. Among my papers I find
a carbon of one of these letters.

17 April 1922

My beloved Friend:

The vacation period brings with it a change of program.
The idea therefore came to me that this week instead of the
usual dissertation I would send you as appropriate to the
Easter season some true New England mayflowers. Ac-
cordingly I arose early this morning and journeyed to
Ponemah.

I have just returned after a day spent in the same place
which we visited eleven years ago. I have wandered through
the chestnut woods where we took lunch and where, but
for your watchfulness, I might have started a forest fire. I
inspected the stone wall where you stood when you let me
take your picture. I sat in the same little station where we
waited for the train. I need not speak of the memories
which these places brought back to me, memories full of
unutterable sorrow for that which might have been. This I
foresaw when I went. But I decided upon Ponemah for two
reasons. I considered that if I wanted flowers to send to you,
there was no better place to look than the one which you
had shown me. I also considered that the lost can sometimes be found in the place where the loss occurred.

As for the flowers, the decision was well justified. It is
true that in the chestnut woods where we spent most of the
day I found only a few scattering clumps and not many
blossoms, and I was beginning to despair. Then I went a
little further down the lane and turned in to the right, and
there, well back from the lane I came upon acres and acres
of open woodland fairly carpeted with arbutus. It was

fully as plentiful as in any place I have found, though the coloring was not perhaps as deep a pink. It is clear that eleven years ago we did not find the best place.

I filled a box with some of the choicest specimens, packing it with damp moss and a few sprays of wintergreen and ground-pine and went back to the station to mail it. There I made a disconcerting discovery. The entire region was quarantined. No trees, shrubs, perennial plants, or greens may be shipped outside of the zone now infested by the gypsy and brown-tail moths, because of the danger of carrying their eggs. I had heard of this but I had forgotten it. At first I thought of sending the box from Boston. Then it came to me that this regulation stood for a principle which I should recognize. It was not easy to accept this view, and coming back I felt sad and desolate. The weather had changed, much as my mood. While in the morning there had been bright sunshine, it was now raining. But as the train drew near to Boston, the clouds lifted and my mood also changed with the thought: "After all, this is as it ought to be."

Then came a hopeful thought. Though I may not send you the few little flowers I have gathered and have sent them to Mother instead—who will get them fresh in the morning—I can tell you of the acres of growing flowers which I have found and of the thought of you which they have brought to me. Though I may not give you as I wish these material tokens, there are other ways in which I can express my love for you which are independent of distance and of time. And though that which might have been can never be recalled, that which still may be will perhaps be better than that which might have been, even as from the beginning it has been my prayer that no desire of mine should be granted which might cause you unhappiness or prove to be not the best.

And so instead of the flowers I wanted to send, I am sending just the assurance of my constant thought and of my complete willingness to express my love for you in whatever way may be right and acceptable to you. And I am wondering if I may not have found to-day a better understanding of you and of the possibilities of our relationship one to the other.

For the coming school year I was faced with a financial problem. The scholarship allowance which had been granted me by Andover Seminary for the previous semester was not renewed. The committee decided that my project did not come within the province of a school of religion. This was a serious matter, for Mother, out of her slender resources, had already gone the limit and beyond in her efforts to help me out. Dean Sperry, however, came to the rescue. He took the matter up with Rev. J. Edgar Park of the Second Church in West Newton and his church advanced the money needed to cover the tuition fees of Harvard's graduate school.

The feature of my academic work that year was Dr. Cabot's seminar at Harvard on the preparation of case records for teaching purposes. I look back upon this as one of the best courses I have ever had. Most of the members were leading social workers from the Boston area—among them Dr. William Healy, Dr. Augusta Bronner, Miss Ida Cannon, and Miss Lucy Wright. It was required of each member that his contribution be submitted two weeks in advance of presentation. It was then mimeographed and given out the week before. When it was then considered by the group, the time was spent not in reading the new material but in exchanging views on subject matter which had been read and in many cases commented on in writing before we assembled.

In the same period I attended Professor McDougall's seminar on theories of mind and body. This seminar provided an interesting contrast to that of Dr. Cabot's in that most of the time was given to the reading of new material. I recall one instance in which one of the students took three successive evenings for the reading of an abstruse paper.

The most time-consuming task in the year of 1923 was the formulation of my project for the study of the interrelationship of religious experience and mental illness for presentation to the Institute for Social and Religious Research, the agency which had taken over the survey findings of the Interchurch World Movement. I had been connected with that agency before my illness, and I was encouraged by them to present my plan. My understanding has been that although the Institute approved the project, the National Committee for Mental Hygiene did not. Under the proposed plan I was to work at the Boston Psychopathic Hospital, taking on cases in which the religious factors were in evidence. Several modifications were made to meet the Institute's criticisms and final decision was delayed until February, 1924.

Meanwhile, in the year 1923-24, I had transferred all my operations, with the exception of Dr. Cabot's seminar, to the Boston Psychopathic Hospital. There I began work in June, 1923, under Dr. Frederick Lyman Wells in psychometrics. However, I came to the conclusion that in our efforts to measure intelligence we were dealing with peripheral rather than with centrally important factors. I therefore transferred to the Social Service Department headed by Miss Susie Lyons. There I found just what I was looking for. I was able to study the entire person in his social setting. In my previous efforts in the making of sociological surveys I had found that it was easy to gather facts and figures on such things as age, sex, race, education, church affiliation, etc., but when it came to the more significant factors, such as motives, values, and religious experience, there we had to stop. We did not dare to ask such questions. But now, as a social worker, going into a home to help a person in need, the social situation opened up in a way which had not been possible when my role was that of a mere inquirer.

Word finally came that my project had been rejected. Dr. Cabot then came to the rescue. He promised to back it himself, and he prepared a letter to send out to his friends, soliciting their support. In this letter he stressed the great need among the neglected mental sufferers, but at the same time he made it very clear that he did not believe that a religious worker could do anything beyond giving comfort and consolation.

The letter was about to be sent out when he called me in. It had come to his attention through Miss Hannah Curtis, the chief of Social Service in the State Department of Mental Disease, that Dr. William A. Bryan of the Worcester State Hospital was willing to try a chaplain. He wanted to know if I would be interested.

Of course I was interested. So also was Arthur Holt, the chief of the Congregational Social Service Commission, whom I had known in Kansas and who four years before had invited me to join his staff. He was at that time considering an offer from the Chicago Theological Seminary. I had had many conferences with him, and he had become much interested in the experiences I was uncovering at the Psychopathic Hospital, so much so that he had commissioned me to make for him a survey of the churches and missions of Boston's Negro section. We had become convinced that the problem of mental health brought a ringing challenge to the Christian Church and that the strategic point of attack lay in the theological schools. We were also convinced that these schools themselves needed overhauling. It seemed to us they had been failing to make use of scientific method in the study of present-day religious experience. We were also impressed by the failure of the psychologists and sociologists and psychiatrists to carry their inquiries to the level of the religious. Here then was a great no man's land which needed to be explored. Therefore he had been talking with me about joining his staff in case he accepted the Chicago offer.

This new opening in Worcester seemed to us both in direct line with the plans we had been considering. He therefore accepted the Chicago offer, and I accepted Dr. Bryan's offer with the understanding that part of my time was to belong to the Chicago Theological Seminary. Our new venture was substantially aided by the Massachusetts Congregational Conference, which contributed six hundred dollars toward the chaplain's salary.

Thus it came to pass that on July 1, 1924, I arrived in Worcester, ready to begin my experiment in the religious ministry to the mentally ill. So far as I am aware, there was at that time only one other full-time chaplain in the mental hospitals of this country, the Rev. Sidney Ussher, who was serving on Ward's Island, in New York City, under the auspices of the Episcopal City Mission Society of New York City.

In undertaking this new assignment I had a clear understanding with Dr. Bryan that I was to come as chaplain and research worker. I was to have no responsibility for such things as recreational activities, library, or post office, and I was to have free access to the case records, the right to visit patients on all the wards, to attend staff meetings where the cases were being discussed, and to be recognized as part of the therapeutic team.

One of my early experiences at Worcester was an encounter with the press. It so happened that at the time I arrived

Worcester's morning newspaper was engaged in writing up the hospital. The reporter wanted a story from me. Dr. Bryan approved but stipulated that I should prepare the copy and let him see it. This I did and then gave it to the reporter. The morning paper used it without change, but the headline writer got busy. In glaring type the morning paper proclaimed, "Worcester Hospital Appoints Soul Healer." And the evening paper rewrote the article on the basis of the headline. Since that time I have been wary of publicity and have made it a policy to rely for publicity upon articles in scientific journals rather than upon newspapers and magazines.

One early attempt of mine at putting my message before the general public was a paper which I entitled "In Defense of Mr. Bryan." It was published in the *American Review*. Taking my departure from the Scopes Trial in Dayton, Tennessee, I cited my studies of church attendance in different regions of the United States (see page 67) to support the proposition that the influence of the church tended to vary inversely with the liberalization of popular religious opinion. The church needed an authoritative message of salvation. This the Fundamentalist churches supplied. Asked what they were trying to do, their leaders would reply in terms of "saving souls," and the revival meeting was their common practical activity. Of course they were giving treatment without diagnosis, but it *was* treatment. The "liberal" churches, on the other hand, were giving neither treatment nor diagnosis. They were defining their task in terms of bringing in the kingdom of God, and the sick of soul they were turning over to the doctors. Their message had thus become apologetic. They were explaining the ancient faith in terms of modern thought, failing to go forward in the task of exploring the field which was distinctively their own.

This paper I had entitled originally "In Defense of Mr. Bryan by a Disciple of Dr. Fosdick." I was careful to exempt Dr. Fosdick himself from the general charge, for he did have a message of salvation for the sick of soul. Nevertheless, when I submitted the paper to him, he said that if I published the paper under that title it would have to be over his dead body. He did agree with me in part, going on to say that much of his message he owed to an experience which had sent him to a mental hospital during his adolescent period.[1]

Sometime that fall of 1924, I was visited by a couple of young men whom I had known at the Episcopal Theological School in Cambridge and with whom I had had many talks. They came to inquire into the possibility of working as attendants in the hospital, with the idea of learning something about mental illness and mental health. So far as I am concerned that was the first suggestion of the idea of clinical pastoral training in its stricter sense. It came, I believe, from Dr. Cabot. As the inaugurator of hospital social work and of the case method in medical education, he was much interested in my undertaking at Worcester, and he had on several occasions talked about it and about the need of a clinical year for students in theology. It was his article in the *Survey Graphic* for September, 1925, which called national attention to the plan.

The general idea was, of course, in line with the ideas upon which Arthur Holt and I had previously agreed, and when, in the spring of 1925, I was appointed as research associate in the Chicago Theological Seminary and went to Chicago to look the situation over, we included clinical training in our plan. On the way back I visited Union Theological Seminary in New York,

[1] Harry Emerson Fosdick, *The Living of These Days* (New York: Harper & Brothers, 1956).

and then Andover and Boston University, with the result that in the summer of 1925 we had four theological students at Worcester. One came as a social worker, one as an understudy for me, so that I might be free to spend the fall quarter in Chicago, and two worked ten hours a day as attendants on the ward. The plan went fairly well in spite of a small setback. One of the ward workers came with the belief that he was taking his life in his hands. I was unaware of his state of mind and had had him placed on an interesting receiving ward. He had been there hardly fifteen minutes when one of the patients ran amok. He brandished a table fork and gave utterance to some high-powered words. My new recruit ran into the clothesroom and locked himself in, leaving the charge attendant to handle the situation alone. It took us a long time to live that down.

Meanwhile, I had been taking full advantage of the permission to write which Alice had given me at the time I left Westboro in 1922. That permission had been a guarded one. She made it clear that she might not reply and that she gave her consent only insofar as it might be of help to me. For about two years I wrote once each week. Then, as my plans began to take shape, I raised the question whether she might not be willing to share in the new task which I saw opening before me. Her reply was sharp and decisive. There was no possibility of such a thing, and the fact that I had read into her permission to write a meaning which was not there made it necessary to withdraw that permission. It was the same sort of letter as the one which had bowled me over in 1912 before I went to Iowa State College, following the one in which she had written of her skill in keeping house and making doughnuts. In my reply I pointed out that this was not an answer I could accept. I had never insisted that her answer must be the one I wanted, but only that it must be one

I could accept as God's answer. It was only because she had denied me such an answer that I continued to hope. I could not and would not give up until that answer had been given. Therefore, I would continue to write, trusting that if I were wrong in this, she would make it clear to me.

She did not correct me, and I continued to write. I even went to the length of writing her each day a report on the day's happenings, a sort of "installment letter," which I mailed to her each week. But the fact remains that on my visit to Chicago in the spring of 1925 she refused to see me, and this refusal was for me a particularly significant one.

On my way back from Chicago I had stopped off at Union Seminary for the purpose of recruiting students. There I had got just one recruit, a young woman of extraordinary ability and charm by the name of Helen Dunbar. She was at that time a middler at Union and was working on a Ph.D. in comparative literature. Her thesis was on "Medieval Symbolism and Its Consummation in the Divine Comedy." I was at once interested, for ever since my decision not to give up hope in my love for Alice, Dante had been for me a sort of patron saint, and I had kept his picture hanging in my room. We found other things in common. She also was interested in languages, and at the age of twenty-two she was conversant with some fifteen languages and dialects. Most important was the fact that she was planning to study psychiatry, and she was enough interested in our project to come and work as an attendant on the wards.

I arranged for her to serve with our Social Service Department. There she did outstanding work, and even though she stayed only one month, she made a contribution which helped greatly in the launching of the project. She was quick to see the significance of what we were trying to do, and she maintained her interest after leaving. Upon me she made a deep impression.

One of the first problems with which I was faced at Worcester was that of finding a hymnal and service book suitable for our patients. A small book of worship printed by the local Episcopal Church for its own evening service was in use when I took over. This provided a service in which the congregation could have a large part, not merely in song but in prayer and response, and the hymns and the psalms which it contained, while few in number, were excellent from the literary standpoint. Therapeutically, however, there was room for improvement. Of the fifteen psalms, six were of the imprecatory type, with all too many references to "enemies," and of the hymns some were actually disturbing. The classic example was the well-known hymn, "O Christian, dost thou see them?" a hymn which evokes all the hallucinations, and calls for action besides. Examination of the available hymnals showed that much of the material they contained was inapplicable to our situation, and some was definitely unwholesome. This was particularly true of the gospel songs so widely used in this country of ours. In most of them, salvation is a matter of the life beyond and is dependent upon the vicarious atonement. This appears as an escape device rather than a summons to the sacrificial way of life.

With the encouragement of the Rev. Henry W. Hobson of All Saints Church in Worcester, I therefore undertook to compile one myself. This book, originally entitled *Lift Up Your Hearts,* is now in its fourth revised edition under the title of *Hymns of Hope and Courage.* It has met with criticism on the ground that it is too "high-brow," but I still believe in the principles on which it is built. I am convinced that words do count and that religious belief is more likely to be affected by the hymns than by the sermons. For mental patients who are grappling desperately with what for them is Ultimate Reality, it is therefore of the utmost importance that the religious service should bring suggestions which are wholesome and constructive. For this reason I have in this book sought to bring together a collection of hymns, prayers, and passages of Scripture which have some claim to inspiration as measured by literary quality, doctrinal validity, and therapeutic effect, a collection from which the inapplicable and the disturbing have been excluded.

Another production of this beginning period was a paper entitled "Personality Changes and Upheavals Arising out of the Sense of Personal Failure." This paper, published in the *American Journal of Psychiatry* of April, 1926, presented a chart which has ever since constituted my own psychiatric classification scheme. It was based upon early case studies at the Boston Psychopathic Hospital and at Worcester, also upon certain cases of religious experience. The distinctive feature of this scheme is the differentiation between chronic mental illnesses, with their insidious onset, and the acute, stormy types. I attempted in this paper to show that the latter may be attempts at reorganization, manifestations of healing power analogous to fever or inflammation in the body, and that, as such, they are closely related to the dramatic types of religious experience.

I had just finished this paper, in the winter of 1925, when I chanced upon Harry Stack Sullivan's "Conservative and Malignant Features of Schizophrenia" in the *American Journal of Psychiatry* of July, 1924. I was deeply interested in this, for it gave needed support to my own views. I wrote to him, therefore, and a little later I went down to see him at the Sheppard and Enoch Pratt Hospital in Baltimore, where at that time he was clinical director. I saw him many times after that, always with increasing respect and affection.

In the fall of 1925 I entered upon my duties as research associate at the Chicago Theological Seminary, going out to Chicago, while Carl Hutchinson, also a research associate in the Seminary who had spent the summer at Worcester, took over my duties at the hospital.

My first assignment at Chicago was the study of a small mining community near La Salle, Illinois. It was an interesting experience, although I cannot claim for it any important results beyond the fact that it served as a first step in establishing the connection with the Chicago Theological Seminary which has been so vitally important to me and to the clinical-training project.

Meanwhile, Arthur Holt had been active. He had shown some of my case studies to Professor Robert E. Park of the sociology department of the University of Chicago. Professor Park was interested. He said they were most unusual, and suggested an approach to the Spelman Fund. This we made, and the Spelman Fund sent a young representative to look us over. A little later we had a visit from Professor W. I. Thomas. My understanding has been that their report was favorable, but that obstacles were encountered. In the first place, the approval of the National Committee for Mental Hygiene was needed, and again this was not forthcoming. The other obstacle was a new development of great importance. The Chicago Theological Seminary became the recipient of a bequest of about three and a half million dollars from the estate of Victor Lawson, the Chicago publisher. Fortunate though this was, it took the edge off our appeal for help from the Spelman Fund.

Many were the dreams which that bequest evoked. So far as I was concerned the chief result was the offer of a position as assistant professor in the social ethics department. This I rejected for the reason that it seemed to me all-important to maintain a hospital base, but I was given the position of research associate and lecturer with professorial standing. Of major importance to our project was the appointment of my old friend, Fred Eastman, to the chair of religious literature and drama, and of Arthur Cushman McGiffert, Jr., to the chair of systematic theology.

In the summer of 1926 we altered our plan of training at the Worcester State Hospital. Dr. Park, of the Second Church in West Newton, who had done much to help us in getting started, sent out a letter to twelve of his fellow ministers in Boston, seeking support. This letter brought in three hundred and fifty dollars. This money we used to pay attendants' wages to two students who came on full time to do recreational work, a service which at that time was not in operation at Worcester. After these appointments had been made, two other theological students were sufficiently interested to join our group and do regular work as attendants. It may be noted that with the advent of students I was glad to find for them opportunities to perform legitimate service which would permit them to study the problem without insisting that this service must be germane to the chaplain's office. I did not propose to bring in novices and turn them loose to do religious or therapeutic work.

The fall of 1926 was for me another eventful period. It brought me my first opportunity to teach in a theological seminary. This meant a lot of hard work of the kind that does not make news. In my teaching I used a case discussion method modeled somewhat after Dr. Cabot's seminar. We used mimeographed case records drawn chiefly from our Worcester laboratory. These were given in advance to the students, along with questions and references. The preparation of the needed material was quite a chore. In addition to my own class there was a joint seminar with Professor Holt in social ethics, and one with Professor McGiffert in theology. These stimulated significant questions and opened up new fields of research.

Once more I found myself a near neighbor of Alice. Still she refused to see me, and still I continued to write. But toward the end of the quarter I changed my policy. This I announced in a letter written on Christmas Day in 1926.

My thoughts to-day go to the problem which has so long been uppermost in my mind, that of the relationship which through all these years has been central for me. What is now the right course for me to follow? I believe that I can see the answer.

For many years my love for you has been the controlling influence in my life. It is for me associated with all that is best and holiest. Out of it has come my call to the ministry. It has been for me not merely the love of a man for a woman, but a love that has been linked with a desperate cry for salvation.

The experience which sent me to Westboro I interpret as the ending of the dependent relationship which was involved. It has left me free and has given me a task that makes life worth living, even though the hope upon which I staked everything is denied.

It has taken me some time to accept this. I have recognized it and at the same time I have clung to you.

It seems to me that the time has now come to end this one-sided relationship. While the privilege of writing has meant very much to me and I give it up with real reluctance and with deep sadness, I feel that there is nothing I can do to make more clear my love for you and my need of you. I therefore rest my case.

My loyalty to you has not changed, nor will it ever change. In ceasing to write to you I shall not cease to keep the daily record which these letters have contained, and I shall seek ever to be true to the Higher Loyalty, as you have always required of me.

I love you and I need you, but I must cease my own striving. This I do with the assurance that whatever is best I may safely leave to you and to Him into whose service my love for you has led me.

Toward the spring of 1927 Helen Dunbar again entered the picture. She had meanwhile won the traveling fellowship at Union Seminary and was now a student at the Yale Medical School. All her leisure time she was using in the study of symbolism, and she wanted to include symbolism which was not medieval. She therefore turned to Worcester. She wanted to know what sort of symbolism we were finding in our acutely disturbed patients, and under what conditions it occurred. She made several trips to the hospital and worked out a questionnaire on schizophrenic thinking. I was more than ever impressed with her swift intelligence, her keen understanding, and her enormous capacity for work. I saw in her an instrument of the finest precision sent to help in the new undertaking.

In the summer of 1927 we again altered our plan at Worcester. We paired the students, each pair doing the work of one attendant. We then raised money from interested friends, so that each student received fifty dollars a month, which at that time was the regular attendant's wage, and claimed half of the student's time for a program of service and of study. This group was an outstanding one. It included Don Beatty with his splendid talents, Aleck Dodd, a true physician of souls, and Mark Entorf, who contributed much to our research program. This group really put our project on the map, so far as the hospital was concerned. Throughout the history of this movement, the students have had an important part in winning recognition of, and support for, our work. Certainly they have done much to make up for my own deficiencies.

During that same summer we had a visit from Frank Buchman, the leader of the "Oxford Group" movement. One of our physicans had attended a "house party" of the Group. There he met a young Englishman whom he invited to the hospital. Shortly thereafter Mr. Buchman received a "guidance" to come along with him. This he did in company with several of the faithful, and we had a sort of house party at the hospital.

In appearance there was nothing striking about Frank Buchman. He impressed us as an ordinary, successful businessman; but he had remarkable persuasive powers. We brought him one morning to the diagnostic staff meeting. When the meeting was over, about nine o'clock, Dr. Bryan, as host, stopped to talk with him. After about half an hour Dr. Hill, our assistant superintendent, strolled in to ask Dr. Bryan a question. He also got interested, and those two busy executives stayed there talking with Mr. Buchman until well past noon! Dr. Bryan said to me the next morning, "I could hardly get to sleep last night for thinking of what that man said to me." Dr. Hill explained that he was fascinated by Buchman's psychiatric understanding and his skill in dealing with individuals, particularly his technique of painting a picture of the fine possibilities he saw in one, and then, perhaps, raising some shrewd question as to what might be blocking the development of those possibilities.

Our students were divided in their reaction. Some were warmly responsive. Others were skeptical, particularly regarding the reliability of the "guidances." We were all struck by Mr. Buchman's lack of interest in the patients and their problems. Not even a promising young student who had become acutely disturbed following his visit to a house party drew more than passing attention from him.

One of our students who had attended the College Conference of the Young Men's Christian Association at Northfield that summer reported that the "Buchmanites" were the only ones there who were active in the personal evangelism which had been such an important feature of the Northfield College Conference at the time I visited it back in 1904. Apparently Frank Buchman was a present-day representative of the evangelism represented by such leaders as Mott and Speer and Henry Wright.

Toward the end of the summer of 1927 Don Beatty expressed his readiness to stay on for a full year in accordance with Dr. Cabot's idea. I shall never forget the consultation with Dr. Cabot which followed this decision. He listened with keen interest. Then he said, "Thus far I've done nothing to help, but I will this year." Thereupon he wrote a memorandum and handed it to me, saying, "Give that to my secretary." What he gave me was an order for one hundred dollars a month. He then offered to take us down to Harvard Square. We went with him to his fine three-car garage and got in the only car he possessed, a 1925 Model T Ford!

Beatty's advent put new vigor into the work of our department. He is one of the most versatile persons I have ever met and one of the most generous with his time and strength. The class prophet, writing in his college annual at Mount Union, Ohio, described him as "a man with a glorious voice, who in twenty years will be doing something different and distinctive." That prophet was right. Beatty's clear, powerful, finely trained voice, his ability as a leader, his clear understanding of the patients and their problems, his effectiveness as a preacher, writer, and executive were all invaluable in getting our new project under way. Among other things, he took hold of the hospital news-sheet which I had started in 1926. I had depended upon typewriter and bulletin board. At his suggestion we purchased an ancient mimeograph. This was soon used extensively not only for the news-sheet but for the duplicating of case records for teaching purposes, which had become all-important in my teaching assignment at the Chicago Theological Seminary. We also worked together in the issuing of a "Hospital Pictorial" during the summer quarter.

The year 1927 saw the beginning of an ambitious project for the neuro-endocrine study of dementia praecox under the direction of Dr. Roy G. Hoskins of the Harvard Medical School. I was at once impressed with Dr. Hoskins and with his attitude and methods, and I conceived the idea of availing myself of his carefully worked up cases for the study of the religious factors in schizophrenic disturbances. Later on, I served for a time on his staff, and for several years he used our students as observers.

In the summer of 1928 we had a group of twelve students, including Beatty and Dodd, who had been with us throughout the year. An outstanding contribution from this group was in the person of Philip Guiles, who stayed with us and had a leading part in the organization of the movement. He was a charming person of farseeing vision and contagious enthusiasm who had much to give.

No account of these early years at Worcester would be complete which did not take account of the seminars which from the beginning were held twice each week in the Trustees' Room during the summer period. In these we discussed the interrelationship between religious experience and mental disorder, and problems related thereto. Dr. Lewis B. Hill, our brilliant young assistant superintendent, was in general charge, and Dr. Bryan himself frequently sat in with us. Others of the hospital staff who gave valuable aid included Dr. Spafford Ackerly and Dr. Henry B. Moyle. These sessions were open to the professional staff, and they elicited much interest. I like to think that our animated discussions had some part in the development of Worcester's ambitious program of research and instruction.

On the 2nd of June in 1928 there came an event of greatest importance to me. For the first time in eight years Alice consented to see me. This happy development was the answer to my letter of Christmas Day, 1926. The response had not come all at once. It was nine months before she replied at all. She then sent me a birthday card. Early in January, 1928, in response to a Christmas letter of mine, I received a full letter from her, then other letters. Then in June we met. She expressed some apprehension over this meeting. "It won't be easy for either of us," she wrote, "and we may not 'have a good time.' But we are neither of us children, and I hope we can adjust to the demands of the situation." I came on from Worcester for the occasion. We met at Marshall Field's and had not the slightest difficulty in recognizing each other. For luncheon we went to the Palmer House. In a letter of June 11, she spoke of deferring her letter until she could be sure that our meeting had been a step taken in the right direction, adding that it had so seemed to her.

Following this meeting we saw each other as often as circumstances and Chicago's vast distances would permit. During the fall quarters of 1928 and 1929 this meant at least every other week, and during the other quarters I was able to find occasion for several visits to Chicago. Usually we had lunch together downtown, and then went to a play or to an opera. There was no lack of things to talk about. She was ready to acknowledge her interest in the clinical-training project, and her suggestions were always helpful, her judgment sound.

On Thanksgiving Day in 1929 we knelt together before the altar in Hilton Chapel and entered into a covenant of friendship, one with the other. Of this she wrote:

THANKSGIVING DAY, 1929.

DEAR ANTON:

You have been very much in my thoughts to-day, both because of these lovely and unusual roses, which I found awaiting me when I reached home, and because of the events of last night. I don't know why I should be any less direct and honest in speaking of something like that, than in uttering words of warning—so I will tell you what perhaps you could see for yourself, that I was profoundly moved by what took place.

I was, and am, thankful for the prayer. I believe that brought us closer together than anything that has ever happened—the fact that we could in one spirit come to God together.

And the little roses you gave me to wear—still fresh on the table —have been a message and a reminder of our covenant, and for the first time in all these twenty-seven years I feel that I can with safety and with entire honesty sign myself—

with real affection,
ALICE.

In the four weeks remaining until my return to Worcester, we saw each other several times and exchanged a number of letters. In one of these, which came shortly after I returned to Worcester, I find the following:

Your installment letter came Monday and your Sunday note arrived yesterday. Before I forget it, let me say—Write Sunday evenings, *if* you want to and *when* you want to, but don't ever feel that it is a custom or rite or anything else that *must* be observed. There should be no "must" in friendship. Links of bondage welded together in the early days of free and eager giving too often become galling later. So be very sure that I make no demands of any kind. You are absolutely free in every way.

A little later in the same letter she wrote, referring to a pin I had given her, one I had brought from Germany:

You must have thought me unappreciative about the pin. You took me so completely by surprise, and I gave expression to my first quick feeling that you must not give me costly gifts. But I want you to know what I think of the pin itself, which is that I consider it one of the most exquisite things I have ever owned. The fire colors in the opal, the delicacy of the carving, the perfect fitness of the onyx setting, all make it so beautiful that I look upon it and say to myself, "Is it really mine?" And it *is mine*, given and accepted as a memento of our covenant of friendship.

During this period our undertaking had been developing finely. Articles under my name had appeared in the major psychiatric and sociological journals and we were making friends in important theological schools.

In the Christmas vacation of 1928 our clinical-training project was presented before the section on religion of the American Sociological Society at their Washington, D.C., meeting. Arthur Holt was the chairman of that section, and Dr. Hill of Worcester read the paper, doing an excellent job. In the course of the animated discussion which followed, I let slip the view that there was much to support the ancient theological doctrine that conviction of sin was a first step in the process of salvation. To many of those present such a view was heresy, and they were not slow in so expressing themselves. I was greatly delighted when Dr. Harry Stack Sullivan, who had come to this meeting at my invitation, arose and defended my position in one of his characteristically keen and witty speeches.

Our summer group increased in number to sixteen. The group picture that year is noteworthy because of the absence of Beatty's face. He had gone as chaplain to the Pittsburgh City Home and Hospital at Mayview to establish a second training center. The group picture is also noteworthy for the first appearance of Carroll Wise's face. He also has made a very important contribution to the cause.

A development of great importance was Philip Guiles's decision to give himself to the cause of clinical training. I first announced this good news to Dr. Cabot at the annual conference of the National Council for Religion in Higher Education at Wells College in 1929. He was as pleased as I was and promised to back our budget to the extent of eighteen hundred dollars. This talk, a delightful one, took place on the evening before the final day, as we lay on the lawn overlooking the lake. The next day each of the interest groups made its report. The group with which I had been meeting embodied in its report one of my pet doctrines, viz., that the sense of guilt is a major factor in mental disorder and that it is essentially a social judgment which the individual accepts and pronounces upon himself. When this report was read, Dr. Cabot stood up straight as a ramrod and stated that he thought it his duty to say that he did not believe there was a word of truth in that report. Happily, however, this conviction of his did not change his attitude toward our undertaking.

The year 1930 brought with it important developments. First among these was the incorporation of the "Council for the Clinical Training of Theological Students." This took place on January 21 in the study of Rev. Samuel A. Eliot at the Arlington Street Church in Boston. The incorporators, in addition to

Dr. Eliot, were Dr. Cabot, president and treasurer; Rev. Henry Wise Hobson, of All Saints Church in Worcester, now bishop of the Episcopal Diocese of Southern Ohio, vice-president; Dr. William A. Bryan, of the Worcester State Hospital; Dr. William Healy, of the Judge Baker Foundation in Boston; Rev. Ashley Day Leavitt, of the Harvard Congregational Church in Brookline, Massachusetts. I was secretary, and Philip Guiles, at whose instance the incorporation had taken place, was field secretary. He was charged with the responsibility of raising money, recruiting students, and opening new centers. At Guiles's suggestion we appointed Helen Dunbar of our own first training group as medical director. As a winner of Union Seminary's traveling fellowship, as a doctor of philosophy and author of a scholarly book on medieval symbolism, as a doctor of medicine just returning from a year's study with the great European psychiatrists, it would have been hard to find any one better qualified. This post she held for fifteen years at no little cost to herself.

In June of that year, 1930, my mother died, and my sister and I took the body back to the old home in Indiana. My indebtedness to Mother cannot be measured. She lived for her children and made every sacrifice in order that they might have their chance to develop. Perhaps her most important characteristic was her faith in us. She was even too careful to leave us free to choose for ourselves. There was thus no word of reproach when I failed to make the grade after graduation in 1897. She acceded at once to my change of profession in 1903, and again in 1908. And finally in 1922, it was her faith in me that made possible the new undertaking. Not only did she back me financially to the limit of her resources, but in the dark days at Westboro she always stood by me, and her beautifully written letters brought their all-important message of comfort and faith.

The fall after her death I did not make my usual visit to Chicago. Instead, I accepted a tempting offer from Dr. Hoskins to serve on his research staff at Worcester. I was to help in abstracting the ward observations and to devote myself more vigorously to my own study of the religious factors in schizophrenia. Meanwhile, the course on religion and mental health at Chicago was given by Dr. Thaddeus Ames. It was understood that I was to return in 1931.

Late in November of 1930 there came a serious setback. I suffered another acute psychotic episode. For this disturbance I do not have the full data which I had for the Westboro debacle. They were not saved this time. But the causative factors are fairly clear. There were complications in my relationship with Alice. The shadow of another, younger woman lay between us. It was a gracious shadow, sanctioned, seemingly, by the idea of the family-of-four, which had been so strangely insistent during the psychotic episodes. This other woman knew about Alice, and Alice knew about her. She had had a part in our meeting of 1928. She was even included in our covenant of friendship. There was no disloyalty to either one. I discussed the situation with Alice, and always I found her wise and helpful. But it was hard to see the way, and I was greatly troubled. The climax came as a delayed reaction following a meeting of the three of us, held at my suggestion, when the finding of the right solution became for me an urgent problem.

As in the previous episodes, the actual disturbance followed a period of intensified absorption and prayer. I was working at the time on the revision of the hymnal and I recall a period of uncontrollable sobbing. It seemed that something which ought to have been, was not to be. I had failed, and the world was in danger. In great distress of mind I started forth in my car. First,

I looked up Phil Guiles and turned over to him the responsibility for the project. Then, following my promptings, I drove to my sister's home in Arlington. From there I went to the home of a cousin in Exeter, New Hampshire; thence back to Boston. There I parked the car and took a train for New York. After a few hours there I returned to Boston and called on Dr. Cabot. Of that visit I recall that I identified with my father, inquiring about myself in the third person. Dr. Cabot was much alarmed and saw to it that I was at once hospitalized.

The ideation, as nearly as I can remember it, was much the same as at Westboro. Something terrible was about to happen. This world of ours was to have become a brilliant star; but something had gone wrong, and it was now to become a Milky Way. I was, it seemed, or should have been, a very important person, and my failure was chiefly responsible for the impending catastrophe. The family-of-four idea was also present. I became aware of new dimensions. Mysterious forces were at work, some of them evil forces which took the form of mice and ran up and down in the spinal column. It was all very terrifying.

Fortunately, the disturbed condition lasted less than three weeks. Then it cleared up. I awakened as out of a bad dream. So far as I can determine, I was none the worse for it. In fact, it solved the problem which had occasioned it. The two women both stood by me, but they could not ignore the seriousness of the disturbance, and my attempt to interpret the family-of-four idea in accordance with my own wishes was definitely ended. This disturbance thus differed from those at Westboro in that the latter were clearly constructive. Painful though they were, they marked a new and creative development. The disturbance of 1930, on the other hand, merely saved me from a situation which should not have arisen. Even though I was myself the better for it, the social effects were in some ways disastrous. There was damage to the project.

Dr. Cabot, the president of the new "Council," was particularly aroused. He had throughout been opposed to the psychogenic interpretation of mental illness. My views now became abhorrent to him. He decreed that I must have nothing to do with the program of instruction. Phil Guiles supported him in this. Dr. Dunbar stood by me and saved the day so far as I was concerned.

Phil Guiles, naturally enough, felt it important to have me out of the way, and he started to raise money from among my friends in order to send me to Europe. Knowing nothing of this, I had meanwhile made arrangements with the Massachusetts Congregational Conference to continue the fifty-dollar-a-month stipend which they had been giving me. I had also secured Dr. Bryan's consent to my staying on in the hospital in order to continue the research project which I had started in collaboration with Dr. Hoskins, and Dr. Hoskins had agreed to let me have a secretary to help with that project. Such a helper I had found in Miss Geneva Dye of the previous summer's training group, and a very efficient, fine person she was. I had also resumed my work on the revision of the hymnal. I could not therefore see my way clear to going to Europe at the expense of my friends when there was so much to be done at Worcester. And I knew very well that if I allowed the research project to get cold, it might never be finished. A difficult situation thus arose.

Nevertheless, the good work went on. At Worcester in the summer of 1931 there were twenty students, and through Guiles's unflagging efforts new centers were opened, one at the Rhode Island State Hospital, under Aleck Dodd; another at the Syracuse Psychopathic Hospital, under William Boehnker and, later, Harold Hildreth. At the same time Guiles himself found time to start a chaplaincy program at the Massachusetts General Hospital.

GROWING PAINS

Because of the complications resulting from my tailspin, it seemed to me better to shift my base of operations from Worcester to the Elgin State Hospital in Illinois, where the superintendent, Dr. Charles F. Read, was already acquainted with our project and ready to respond. Such a shift had the advantage of making possible a closer relationship with the Chicago Theological Seminary, which from the beginning had sponsored my work. More than that, Chicago with its nine Class A theological schools, was the center of theological education in the Middle West, if not in the country.

Not least among the considerations in my own mind was the fact that Chicago was Alice Batchelder's home, and in this new setting I continued to see her as often as her duties and her health permitted. She had been since 1919 a "working girl," employed as chief of the credit section of the Continental-Illinois Bank, with a weekday schedule which required geting up at six, hurrying off to work at seven-thirty, back home at six, with dinner and housekeeping to take care of. Her little leisure time in the evening was used in reading to the "girls" who shared her apartment and in lessons in journalism or creative writing. Her Sundays were taken up with church in the morning and an "at home" to visitors in afternoon and evening. Her duties were augmented by the fact that the third member of the little household had become a helpless invalid. I saw her usually about once a month, when we took dinner downtown or went together to the opera, to an occasional play, or out for a drive in Chicago's sub-urbs—meetings which are precious memories to me.

The transfer to Elgin was made on April 1, 1932, and that summer we opened the new training center with a group of nine students, an outstanding group which helped splendidly to get things started right.

We began with a vigorous program of service, similar to that at Worcester. The first step was the transfer of the service of worship from the afternoon to the morning. This made it possible for patients to attend without fear of missing their visitors, and the average attendance at once doubled. A second step was the organization and training of a vested choir of patients to replace the hired soloist from downtown. This made possible the type of service I wanted to develop. A third step was the organization of an intramural softball league, made up of patients, in place of the semiprofessional baseball team composed chiefly of play-ers from downtown. Then on the Fourth of July and Labor Day we held play festivals similar to those I had staged at Westboro. In order to promote these activities we issued each week a mimeo-graphed news-sheet called the *Messenger,* and during the sum-mer we supplemented this with a *Pictorial* similar to the one that had been published at Worcester. The students not only helped with these activities but they worked on the wards as at-tendants sixteen hours a week.

With Elgin's five thousand patients this was a heavy program, but we found it rewarding. The work on the wards and the recreational activities provided normal contacts with the patients and gave us unrivaled opportunities to serve and to observe. Each student was required to submit written observations day by day and to work up, intensively, at least one case. Such findings, together with selected readings, were then discussed in our group conferences. Not least in importance was the privilege of attending the hospital's regular clinical staff conferences.

This full program was of course possible only in the summer period, but two of the group, Rothe Hilger and Ronald Frederickson, felt the challenge sufficiently to stay on for a full year. With their help we continued the program in reduced form for the rest of the year.

In addition to the program of service and of instruction, I found time to continue my program of inquiry, and the first year at Elgin saw the publication of work already done before I left Worcester. My "Problem of Values in the Light of Psychopathology" appeared in the *American Journal of Sociology* of July, 1932, and the second edition of the hospital hymnal appeared under the title of *Hymns of Hope and Courage* instead of *Lift Up Your Hearts*. This revision was a drastic one. As in the case of the first edition, it was made possible by the generosity of friends. Cecil Smith, assistant professor of music at the University of Chicago and assistant professor of religious music at the Chicago Theological Seminary was the music editor.

In the summer of 1933 we had a group of eleven students, with Victor Schuldt and his wife, a talented couple, staying on for a full year. One of the major events of that year, from my standpoint, was the publication in the *American Journal of Psychiatry* of my "Experiential Aspects of Dementia Praecox." This thirty-three-page article contained the results of the study I had made at Worcester in collaboration with Dr. Hoskins in his research on the neuro-endocrine factors in dementia praecox. I was able to show in this study that religious concern tends to be associated with the reactions of *anxiety* and *self-blame* and that the outcome in such reactions is relatively favorable. In sharp contrast, the reactions of *drifting* tend toward progressive disintegration, and those of *delusional misinterpretation* eventuate generally in stabilization on an unsatisfactory basis. A feature of this study is the attention given to schizophrenic ideation, and the finding that acute schizophrenic reactions tend to be associated with a characteristic constellation of ideas. This study provided the basis for a book, on which I had already begun work.

In the summer of 1934 there were sixteen students in our training program, and a really notable group it was, with Francis McPeek, Wayne Hunter, and Fred Kuether all throwing in their lot with the Council for Clinical Training. The latter two stayed on through the year of 1934-35.

The Council, under the active leadership of Dr. Dunbar and Dr. Hill, was looking up that year. Two memorable conferences were held, one in New York and the other in Philadelphia. The former I shall long remember. Dr. Cabot, as president, was to give the keynote paper at our evening meeting, but on our arrival in New York we were told that he would be unable to attend because of the serious illness of his wife. However, that evening he was there and gave his paper. His wife had died that morning, but he had immediately left for New York, saying that was what she would have him do. That paper was the nucleus of *The Art of Ministering to the Sick,* the book which he and Russell Dicks put out together.

Some three months later, Dr. Cabot used that same paper in the Alden-Tuthill Lectures at the Chicago Theological Seminary. He had by this time expanded it to three lectures, one of which was entitled "The Wisdom of the Body." In that unforgettable lecture he described the marvelous devices employed by the body in maintaining and restoring health. In talking with him afterward, I ventured to suggest that I was interested in the attempt to find the analogous processes in the human mind. Dr. Cabot shook his head emphatically and replied that he believed thoroughly in the wisdom of the body, but not in that of the mind.

The summer of 1935 brought together in our training program another outstanding group, nineteen in number. Especially important was the presence of Don Beatty, who had been forced to leave Pittsburgh, after six years of distinguished service, because of a political upset which had ousted his superintendent. The end of the summer found Beatty, Hunter, and McPeek staying on. A stronger combination it would have been hard to find.

On August 24, 1935, I received a note from Alice, saying that she was going into retirement for an operation and that the edict had gone forth, "No callers, no flowers." I discovered soon that the difficulty was cancer and that the outlook was hopeless.

I was working at the time on the dedication of my *Exploration of the Inner World,* which was about ready to go to press. It had long been my intention to dedicate this book to her, and I now became wholly absorbed in the task of writing this dedication. I began to see things from her standpoint. How often I had disappointed her! What poor use I had made of our friendship, failing in these later years to reach the deeper levels of understanding! And now she was leaving! Then I was carried away into an abnormal condition and some of the ideas I had had in Washington in 1908 came flooding back (see p. 59). Once more I saw myself as a wretch in direst need upon whom she had taken pity. Again I had the idea that this earth should have become a brilliant star, but something had gone wrong and instead it would become only a Milky Way. I recall identifying myself with my father, and feeling that he was getting old and would be unable to carry on much longer.

Fortunately, Beatty and McPeek and Hunter were quick to recognize the signs of trouble and there was no disruption of the social situation. They guarded me carefully, and on November 11 they spirited me away to the Sheppard and Enoch Pratt Hospital in Baltimore so quietly that scarcely anyone in Elgin knew about it. I was there on December 2, at the time of Alice's death. About two weeks later I was able to return and resume my teaching at the Seminary before the end of the quarter. Once more the disturbance had cleared up within four weeks. I look upon this episode as another problem-solving experience. Its meaning I find in the clarification of my relationship with Alice.

My *Exploration of the Inner World* was published in 1936. It had visited the editorial offices of eight different publishers before Willett and Clark finally accepted it. The following year was marked by two series of conferences, both of which grew out of the publication of this book. The first of these was held at the home of Professor McGiffert, with a selected group of specialists in psychiatry, psychology, anthropology, sociology in attendance. The other, for ministers in the Chicago area, was held under the auspices of the Chicago Council for Clinical Training in the La Salle Street building of the Young Men's Christian Association. In each series the discussions centered upon some case study.

The striking thing brought out at the interdisciplinary conferences was the reluctance of the theologians to recognize any obligation of theirs in the province of mental illness. Rather to my surprise, the chief opposition came from Professor Henry Nelson Wieman of the Chicago Divinity School. He recognized that Augustine W., the patient whose case I had used in the first chapter of my *Exploration,* had some religious ideas, but he saw no significance in that fact. What were those ideas but verbalizations taken over from the environment? All of us, he held, make use of an accepted currency of ideas. If this is true of normal persons, how much more so of psychotics! Dr. David Slight, of the University of Chicago, who represented the psychiatrists, took the position that the trouble with most of the mentally ill is that they are trying to be too good and that his job as a physician was to make them live dogs rather than dead lions.

On November 29, 1937, a conference on the present-day status of the psychology of religion was held at the Quadrangle Club with Professor Edmund S. Conklin of Indiana University as speaker. The picture presented was not roseate. Professor Conklin was impressed with the high hopes which had prevailed in the first decade of the century, when William James, Stanley Hall, George A. Coe, Edwin D. Starbuck, and James Bisset Pratt were vigorously active, and all were looking forward enthusiastically to a new day in the study of religion. But in 1937, he said, if a graduate student in any of our major universities were to offer a doctoral thesis in the psychology of religion, it would not be accepted. With this view Professor Carr and Professor Kingsbury of the psychology department of the University of Chicago both agreed.

Early in 1938 there came an important change in my situation. I was brought in to the Chicago Theological Seminary to give full time to writing and teaching, while Beatty took over as chaplain at the Elgin State Hospital under an arrangement whereby he gave two days a week to teaching at the Seminary.

During this period, at Arthur Holt's suggestion, I undertook a study of the Pentecostal sects which had been growing so rapidly during the 1930's. My task was to find out if they were really growing as fast as reported, and if so, why? What could we learn from them? This study was financed by the Congregational Council for Social Action and, later, by a grant-in-aid from the Social Science Research Council. In this study I sought to tie into the survey work I had done some thirty years before and also to apply to living religious experience the insights derived from my work at the hospital. Following my usual plan, I chose certain counties as sample areas within which I could see the Pentecostal groups in their setting. In the course of this study, I made surveys of Coles County, Illinois; Monroe and Lawrence counties in Indiana; Gibson County, Tennessee; Stone and Vernon counties in Missouri; Lee County, Alabama; and Chester County, South Carolina. I also made brief surveys of Springfield, Missouri; Princeton and Richmond, Indiana; and Athens, Ohio. I drew also upon my earlier study of Roxbury, Massachusetts, which I had made in 1924 for Dr. Holt while at the Boston Psychopathic Hospital (see p. 149).

This study brought out the somewhat surprising fact that the economic depression of the 1930's had not been marked by any demonstrable increase in mental illness, but it had resulted in a considerable degree of religious quickening among the underprivileged classes, upon whom the strains fell most heavily. I found the explanation in the fact that in facing economic hardship, these people had reacted in accordance with the Christian principles in which they had been reared. Instead of blaming others and seeking to change the social order, they took stock of their own shortcomings, and thinking and feeling together about the things which matter most, they came through with a deepened sense of fellowship and a religious faith which came alive for them. The Pentecostal groups thus represented the creative phase of organized religion, and with all their weaknesses and crudities, they may be regarded as manifestations of healing power.

Late in 1938 and early the following year I had several pleasant visits with my old Forest Service chief, Raphael Zon. He was at this time director of research for the Forest Service's North Central Region, with headquarters at the University of Minnesota. He was also engaged in helping Gifford Pinchot write his autobiography. On one of his trips East he stopped off and met with some of the faculty members at the University of Chicago. We questioned him particularly regarding his concepts of social ecology, which he had formulated back in 1906, some time before the sociologists had taken it up. We also quizzed him regarding his impressions of Russia, which he had revisited shortly before in connection with an international forestry congress. His knowledge of Russian life and language, his personal acquaintance with some of his Russian fellow-revolutionaries, including Kerenski and Lenin, enabled him to speak with some authority, and we were all impressed with his fairness and breadth of view. One of the principles upon which he insisted was that any person and any nation should be judged by what it is in process of *becoming*, rather than by what it *now is*. From that standpoint, he was impressed by the enormous improvement in Russia in the matter of education and industrial development. He was also convinced that the Russian people were pretty solidly behind their government and that there had been tragic misunderstanding in this country of everything having to do with Russian relations.

During my period of residence at the Seminary, I wrote a number of articles for scientific periodicals, four of which appeared in *Psychiatry*. This journal was edited by my friend, Dr. Harry Stack Sullivan, as an attempt at synthesization and cross-fertilization within the related fields of psychiatry, sociology, anthropology, and psychology. My "Types of Dementia Praecox," which appeared in 1938, was a study in psychiatric classification. It called attention to the wide discrepancy in the prevailing concepts of schizophrenic subtypes. I stressed the importance of giving more attention to this problem as one of the growing points in psychiatric theory, but so far as I can discover the only result was that one or two states stopped publishing their statistics regarding these subtypes.

My "Form and Content of Schizophrenic Thinking" was published in *Psychiatry* in 1942. It had its inception in the observation that current discussions of this problem were failing to take account of these schizophrenic subtypes. I pointed out that the term "schizophrenia" is applied to four distinct reaction patterns and that most of the so-called "schizophrenic productions" are best explained as reflections of the fragmentation which so often characterizes defeated persons.

Two articles appeared in the *Journal of Religion*. "The Problem of Sin and Salvation in the Light of Psychopathology" was written for presentation before the regional meeting of the American Theological Association, and "Divided Protestantism in a Midwestern County" was presented before the American Association of Theological Schools at Lexington, Kentucky. The latter was a study of Monroe County, Indiana, where I had grown up.

In 1940 Professor E. A. Ross, of the University of Wisconsin, got the idea of adding a book on the sociology of religion to his sociological series. He had been impressed by the fact that sociologists were not paying enough attention to the phenomena of religion. He therefore approached me, and after two conferences and a good bit of correspondence, I worked out an outline which met with his "full approval." Unfortunately, however, his publisher did not agree. He felt that any book in the field of religion fell outside the limits of profitable activity for his firm. Meanwhile, I had become sufficiently interested to go ahead with it anyway. Professor Holt then suggested that I collaborate with him and with Samuel Kincheloe of the Seminary's sociology department in a book on which they were both already working. We spent about a year on this, when Holt's sudden death brought our plans to an end.

The year 1942 brought me to the age of retirement. It also brought this country of ours into another great war, and Don Beatty enlisted as chaplain in the Air Force. This left a vacancy at Elgin to which I was once more called. I went there in September with the understanding that I would be free to accept the Earl Lectureship at the Pacific School of Religion during the winter quarter. This invitation had come to me through its president, Arthur Cushman McGiffert, Jr., whose support has meant so much to me and to the clinical-training movement. I was able to accept it with the help of Philip Schug, a student of mine at the Seminary who had been serving an interneship under Beatty at the hospital. He carried on during my absence.

In March, 1943, I returned to Elgin in time to bring together, with the help of Fred Kuether, a group of twelve students, among them Tom Klink and Lennart Cedarleaf, who are now, in 1960, leaders in the Council, and Carl Stromee, who stayed on for two years. Kuether, meanwhile, had accepted the chaplaincy of the Illinois Training School for Boys at St. Charles, twelve miles from Elgin, and his presence there added immeasurably to the strength and interest of our teaching program.

The chief event on my calendar in 1944 was a study of conscientious objectors, which I undertook at the request of the Brethren Service Committee. They had met with a puzzling problem. In spite of earnest efforts to develop in their service groups a spirit of good will and co-operation, some of their units, especially those of the camps, had been showing an amazing amount of hostility toward leaders whom they themselves had chosen. What was the reason for this, and what should be done about it? These were the questions they wanted answered.

After an intensive study of one of the camps, and brief visits to other units, most of them in mental hospitals, where I found among the "C.O.'s" a very different spirit, I arrived at the conclusion that many of the C.O.'s were *constitutional* objectors, rather than *conscientious* objectors, and that objectors of the constitutional variety, because they were troublemakers, tended to accumulate in those camps which served as distributing centers because they were not in demand. This study was published in *Psychiatry,* and it attracted some attention.

In our group at Elgin that summer there were nineteen students, among them Granger Westberg and Jesse Ziegler. These two came for short periods, but they have had an important place in the movement. Westberg is now serving as professor of religion and health in the medical school of the University of Chicago and also in Chicago's Federated Theological Faculty, a position which is thus far unique. Ziegler is on the staff of the American Association of Theological Schools.

The outstanding feature of our programs in the summer of 1944 was a visit from Dr. Harry Stack Sullivan. While in Washington on the conscientious objector study, I learned that he was going to New Mexico in July, and I prevailed upon him to stop off at Elgin. As the time of his visit approached, I wrote to him, asking him to let me know when he would arrive, and by what train. I received no reply and I did not know what to do. Finally, on the morning of the appointed day, I received a telephone call. Dr. Sullivan was waiting in the Baltimore and Ohio Station in Chicago, forty miles away. I hurried in and found him pacing nervously up and down, holding by the leash one of his favorite cocker spaniels, and with two heavy bags piled up on the side. I was certainly glad I had not suggested that he take the interurban train! He gave two splendid lectures at our hospital and a superb demonstration of his technique of interviewing patients.

This same year of 1944 saw an event of great importance in the development of clinical training as a national movement. A conference was suggested, and made possible, by Philip Guiles, who for twelve years had been serving as professor of pastoral psychology at the Andover-Newton Theological School in Massachusetts. He proposed this conference in order to further a meeting of minds among those concerned in this field of interest and to explore the relationship of such training to the curriculum of the theological schools. This conference was held in the Western Theological Seminary in Pittsburgh just prior to the biennial meeting of the American Association of Theological Schools. Some thirty representatives of the theological schools were present, together with twenty-nine representatives of the various clinical training agencies. This conference was under the direction of Seward Hiltner, at that time executive secretary of the Commission on Religion and Health of the Federal Council of Churches, and previously director of the Council for Clinical Pastoral Training, whose devoted and efficient service as organizer, writer, and teacher has been a most important factor in the spread of the movement.

In the summer of 1945 I was given a new assignment, that of educational consultant to the Council for the Clinical Training of Theological Students, and William Andrew took my place as chaplain at the Elgin State Hospital. I was to give all my time during the summer to the fourteen different training centers at that time in operation, giving them such help as they might be ready to accept. It was a challenging opportunity, one which gave me a chance to take another look at the movement which I had helped to start some twenty years before.

I discovered quickly that the other centers had been developing along lines different from those which Beatty and I had followed. Most of them at that time were still using my case records as a basis for some of their case discussions, but increasing attention was being given to the techniques of interviewing and to verbatim transcripts of interviews rather than to case histories. This development had originated in the general hospital setting, where students could not be turned loose on the wards without the closest supervision. I saw in this an important contribution. My only question had to do with the lessened interest in case histories. Might it not mean a lessening of interest in the basic understanding of the experiences involved?

I was also somewhat troubled by the genetic emphasis. English and Pearson's *Common Neuroses of Children and Adults* was the law and the gospel in most of the centers. It was assumed that most of the difficulties in later life were due to something which had happened before the fourth year of childhood. There was therefore much speculation about the "oral" and "anal" and "genital" stages of development. I even heard suggestions about the "intra-uterine" and the "intratesticular stages"; and there were some who undertook to explain George Fox in terms of toilet training. The significance of the experience which had brought the patient to the hospital, the frustration out of which it grew, and the type of reaction it represented, were sometimes practically ignored or treated as matters of secondary concern, while the dynamic factors with which religion is primarily concerned were being left in some of the centers for a three-hundred-question barrage at the end of the course.

This meant that there was a tendency to accept Freudian doctrine on authority without scrutinizing it closely, and a failure to ask the questions which are of first importance to the student of religion. What is more, there was no attempt to develop methods of co-operative inquiry which would stand up under criticism nor to build up a body of tested and organized experience. The movement as a whole was not being undergirded by the program of inquiry which seemed to me so important.

I was especially troubled by a tendency to accept the easy solutions to some of the perennial problems of sin and salvation. Take, for example, a patient who is torn with conflict between the demands of conscience and his erotic desires and impulses. The solution offered by some of our chaplain-supervisors was that of getting rid of the conflict by lowering the conscience threshold. There were even those who accepted the later teachings of Wilhelm Reich, advocating a freedom quite at variance with the basic insights of the Hebrew-Christian religion.

Another difficulty which I encountered lay in the prevailing concepts of "group dynamics." According to the current views, good teaching must be "student-centered," never "content-centered," and the teacher himself an umpire rather than an explorer and guide. I had difficulty in adapting myself to the view that the teacher should remain passive. I had a lead which I was trying to follow out, a theory which I was trying to establish or disprove, one which seemed to me important. There was need, it seemed to me, for co-operative inquiry among a considerable number of workers, and for teachers who could lead the way.

I was also troubled by the failure to win more acceptance among the theological schools. From the beginning of this undertaking I had constantly insisted that we were not trying to introduce anything new into the already overcrowded theological curriculum. On the contrary, we were trying to call attention back to the age-old problems of sin, of salvation, of prophetic inspiration. What was new was the approach. In a time when students of religion were making little use of the methods of science, and scientists were failing to carry their inquiries to the level of the religious, we were seeking to make empirical studies of living human documents, particularly those in which men were breaking or had broken under the stress of moral crisis. We were proposing to alter the basic structure of theological education. In 1945, it seemed to me that we had made little progress toward that objective. Where we had found our way into the theological schools, it was chiefly in the form of added courses in "personal counseling," and for the most part we were operating independently of the seminaries.

What made the situation hard for me was the fact that Elgin at once became the stronghold of the tendencies to which I objected. My successor was an able, attractive person with a mind of his own. Since I also had ideas that were dear to me, and since I had no choice but to live at Elgin, where all I had was invested, I was faced with a difficult situation, which I did not handle well. Largely because of the difficulties on the home base, I failed to make the further contribution to the training program which I might otherwise have made.

Since 1945 most of my time has been spent at Elgin. Part of that time I have served as acting chaplain, but my chief contribution has probably been in the writing I have done.

During the period from 1945 to 1947, except for the summer months, I was set free to finish some needed tasks. Chief among these was the editing and mimeographing of the case studies which I had worked up for teaching purposes over the years. I selected and arranged them so that they would represent the different ways employed by patients in dealing with the sense of guilt and frustration. I then bound them, together with questions, references, and comments into a volume under the title of *A Beginning Course in Religion and Mental Health.* A companion volume is entitled, *Collected Papers on Religion and Mental Health.* This second volume consists of excerpts, translations, and summaries of readings which have meant most in my own thinking. These mimeographed volumes have been used not only at Elgin but in other training centers.

To this period belongs also an article on "Co-operative Inquiry in Religion," which appeared in *Religious Education* in September, 1945. This is a study of the journals in the field of religion. It shows the paucity of journals in this field which can lay claim to scientific standing. And even in those we do have, empirical studies of human nature and of religious experience are conspicuous by their absence.

In 1946 my *Problems in Religion and Life* appeared under the imprint of the Abingdon-Cokesbury Press. This book was designed as a manual for pastors. It contains outlines for the study of personal experience in social situations, together with references and interpretations of the different types of maladjustment and various general problems, such as principles of personal counseling, religious education, religion of the underprivileged etc. This book covers the ground I have myself traversed in my attempts at an empirical approach to the study of religion. It also exemplifies the methods I have employed.

An article which I regard as of some importance is my "Onset in Acute Schizophrenia." This appeared in *Psychiatry* in 1947. It is based upon an unusually interesting case, one in which the constructive features of acute schizophrenia are clearly in evidence, and the similarities between auditory hallucinations and creative thinking are readily apparent. This case has been borrowed by other authors, and I have used it elsewhere myself.

With the departure of Chaplain Andrew in November, 1947, to accept a more lucrative offer in the New Hampshire State Hospital, I took over as acting chaplain at Elgin and attempted to launch a research program of the type which seemed to me so much needed. I undertook to inquire into the religious factors in schizophrenia, appealing for a grant-in-aid to the United States Public Health Service and hoping for support from our Council for Clinical Training, which under Fred Kuether's able leadership had taken on new life. This aid did not materialize, but I went on with the project nevertheless.

My reason for going on with the project in the face of the Council's negative attitude is given in a letter to Fred Kuether of October 15, 1947:

The plan which I submitted in my last letter represents my idea of what is now most needed for the advancement of the cause which is entrusted to us. The movement will, I think, stand or fall according to the extent to which it is undergirded with an adequate program of research. This means that we should begin some actual research project and that we should be training men able to carry on. I am of course much disappointed that the project was not approved by the Public Health Service—we missed out, I am told, by a very narrow margin. Their approval would have simplified matters. Let me therefore repeat that my offer to serve as acting head was merely a stop-gap conditioned upon our being able to use the present chaplain's salary to establish the suggested fellowships. I am hoping that after a year or so we may be able to find support from some foundation and that I may be relieved of my responsibilities. In any case, to be worth while this project ought to have the backing of the Council.

A subsequent letter to Fred Kuether clarifies the situation somewhat further.

There is indeed a difference in our philosophy of teaching. While I by no means agree that I am uninterested in my students, I do acknowledge that my emphasis has been more upon the understanding of the patients than upon the personal counseling of students. I proceeded upon the assumption that in dealing objectively with persons in trouble, trying to see their problems in the light of his own reactions, the student gets help in the understanding of his own difficulties. It has been my policy to let the student work out his own problems except in so far as he comes to me for help.

The chief difference, as I see it, lies in your view that inquiry into the religious aspects of mental illness is a secondary matter and that research and training are to be kept separate. According to my philosophy, in all good teaching, student and teacher alike are engaged in co-operative inquiry, and the best possible conditions are to be found when they are actually engaged in a project of some practical significance.

Perhaps you will see what I am trying to say. I have no quarrel with the present training program. The Council is doing good work and I can say, "More power to it." At the same time I fail to see that what you now call "training" must remain the only kind of training. I would therefore claim for training in research as much of a place as getting analyzed, and for tested religious insights as much attention as Freudian doctrine.

With the approval of the superintendent, the chaplain's modest salary was divided between two "research fellows," one of them a young physician, Dr. George H. Stevens, and the other a young clergyman, Rev. Gordon J. Chambers. Together we carried on the routine work of the department—the Sunday morning services, the choir, the group therapy conferences, the editing of a hospital news-sheet, officiating at burial services, calling on the patients in the wards, and attending the staff clinical conferences. We had also a small group of students. Basic to the research project was the making of case analyses of newly admitted patients. Unfortunately Dr. Stevens was called into military service before the project really got under way.

In the spring of 1949 the Council came to terms with us, and with its help we brought together an unusually able group of students. This group undertook a pilot study of the religious factors in schizophrenia along the lines of my research project.

The heavy burden of routine work left little time for writing, but I did attempt to formulate the principles upon which a hymnal for use in hospitals should be constructed, and I began the task of revising our *Hymns of Hope and Courage* in accordance with these principles. The chief feature of this fourth edition is a sixteen-page supplement, consisting chiefly of old favorites which did not fit into our original plan but had value because of their associations. At the same time, we sought to perfect the main text as a collection of the most helpful hymns and singable tunes. Frederick Marriott, the organist of the Rockefeller Memorial Chapel of the University of Chicago, was music editor. Under his direction we completed the task of lowering the pitch of the tunes to meet the requirements of unison singing by the congregation. This revision was made possible by the generosity of friends in commemoration of the twenty-fifth anniversary of the clinical-training movement.

In the winter of 1950, in accordance with my understanding with the Council, I relinquished the chaplaincy, and Herman Eichorn, now of the Napa State Hospital in California, took over. This left me free to finish the revision of the hymnal and to begin work on the study we had made in 1949 of mystical identification in mental disorder.

In October, 1950, the Council celebrated its twenty-fifth anniversary with meetings that were held at the Chicago Theological Seminary and at the Quadrangle Club of the University of Chicago. There were some fifty persons in attendance. In spite of our differences, I was given a central place in this affair, and several articles of mine were reprinted in the *Journal of Pastoral Care.*

Two or three weeks later I went to Augustana Hospital for a checkup by my physician, Dr. Earl Garside. I was expecting to stay one night. Actually I stayed eight weeks, and then spent three months more convalescing at Elgin. An emergency operation had been followed by severe thrombo-phlebitic complications. By May, however, I had recovered sufficiently to attend the annual meeting of the American Mental Hospital Chaplains Association in Cincinnati, where I delivered a paper on the "Therapeutic Significance of Anxiety." This was published in the summer issue of the *Journal of Pastoral Care.*

In August, 1951, when Chaplain Eichorn left for the Napa State Hospital, and no promising successor was in sight, I was again authorized by Superintendent Steinberg to take over as acting chaplain, and for three years the routine duties of the chaplain's office absorbed most of my time and strength. In these

I was assisted, especially in the summer, by a succession of students who gave help, and at the same time required time and attention. I was also aided by two very capable patients. One of them, Miss Virginia Gore, assumed complete charge of our *Messenger* and is now one of our employees; the other, Mrs. Margaret Iannelli, a talented artist, has given twenty years of devoted service to the chaplain's office.

I did, however, find time to do some writing. First among my literary efforts in this period was the completion of my study of *Mystical Indentification in Mental Disorder*. This was delivered before the Central Conference of American Rabbis at Sinai Temple, in Chicago, in December, 1951. It was published in *Psychiatry* in August, 1952. This article is a reconnaissance survey. Its statistics are of the compass-and-pacing variety, so familiar in Forest Service days. A factor analysis was therefore suggested by my friend, Dr. R. L. Jenkins, chief of research, of the Veterans Administration. This was carried out by Dr. Maurice Lorr, statistician with the Veterans Administration, and published in the *Journal of Clinical Psychology* for October, 1954, under the title of "Schizophrenic Ideation as Striving Toward the Solution of Conflict." The formidable statistics do not, however, alter the fact that it is a pilot study. It raises questions and suggests a method of answering them. The questions it raises are important: What are the conditions under which we find the ideas of being Christ, or God, or agents of the superhuman? What are the chances of recovery in such cases? What light do such cases throw upon the experiences of the great prophets and religious leaders?

I therefore supplemented this study by an article on "What Did Jesus Think of Himself?" This was published in the *Journal of the Bible and Religion* for January, 1952. It is a reworking of my attempt to deal with the Messianic claim of Jesus as given in Chapter Four of my *Exploration of the Inner World*. This attempt had been given little or no attention from New Testament scholars. Since my *Exploration* had been out of print for some years, it seemed to me to be in order to make a new attack upon this problem in the light of the study just completed.

Starting with Albert Schweitzer's view that Jesus did think of himself as the divinely appointed Messiah of the Jews, I pointed out that according to the Gospel sources he had not only the ideas of being the Messiah together with that of the imminent coming of the kingdom of God, but he had also ideas of death, of rebirth, and of prophetic mission. This meant, according to my view, that he had the entire constellation of ideas which are characteristic of the acutely disturbed schizophrenic, and these ideas are so deeply embedded in the Gospel sources that we cannot rule them out. What is needed is recognition of the significance of such ideas and of the experiences in which they are found. Even the patient who thinks of himself as Christ or God may be groping after a true insight. We are all of us more important than we dream. The decisive consideration regarding Jesus is that if he did descend into hell, as the Apostles' Creed says he did, he emerged victorious, with insights that enabled him to speak as one who had authority regarding the laws of the spiritual life.

Schweitzer held that only when we recognize that Jesus did think of himself as the Messiah will we ever be able to understand him. In this article I tried to show that Schweitzer was right and, more than that, only as we recognize that Jesus shared in the searching experiences in which these ideas so often appear, will we be able to find the key to the understanding of the profounder struggles of the human soul.

In 1955 my *Religion in Crisis and Custom* made its long-awaited appearance. This is the book which I began in 1940, at the suggestion of Professor Ross, and the one in which Arthur Holt was to have collaborated. As originally planned, it was to have been a larger book, with several chapters devoted to the great world religions. As it now stands, it is based almost entirely upon my own direct observations, and it represents my own methodology. I have tried in this book to carry the leads derived from my studies of personal crisis into the wider field of social crisis and the problems relating to the development and validation of religious faith and its perpetuation and re-creation. From the methodological standpoint, it is a reconnaissance survey whose scale of accuracy is suited to the material under consideration and the yardsticks at my disposal. It breaks new ground and I believe that it has real importance, but the manuscript was sent to the offices of more than thirty publishers before it finally saw the light of day. The fact that it is a cross-frontier study involving religion caused many publishers to shy away from it. What I regard as the book's chief claim to consideration was apparently a handicap in their eyes.

During the past five years I have been taking things somewhat easy under the title of "chaplain emeritus," while Clarence Bruninga, a promising young graduate of Wartburg Seminary, is serving as chaplain at the Elgin State Hospital. I am happy in the fact that he is doing a competent job, both as pastor and teacher. I am happy also in the growth of the movement for the clinical training of students for the ministry. For this I claim no special credit for myself. It has been the work of many persons and it is due to complex forces. Sometimes I have felt that it has gone forward in spite of rather than because of what I have done. It has gone forward under its own power, developing a philosophy which differs not a little from mine. For this I can be thankful, so long as it concerns itself with the living human documents of persons in trouble.

The following credo, which I offered at the Twenty-Fifth Anniversary Conference of the Council for Clinical Pastoral Training held at the University of Chicago in October, 1950, may serve to summarize the central convictions which have grown out of my efforts to deal with the problem of mental disorder in myself and in others:

I believe that man is born subject to human frailties and perversities. Educators may learn much from the consequences of mistakes made in early training, but it is a serious mistake to place all the blame for later maladjustments upon the parents. Even in the best of families and with the best of training unruly desires derived from our animal ancestry are likely to manifest themselves. The garden of the heart when left uncultivated is always taken over by weeds.

I believe that men have divine potentialities. The characteristic feature of human nature is social control through the internalization of social norms within one's self in the form of conscience. The human being has thus the capacity for doing the right thing not through blind instinct or outward compulsion but through inner self-direction. This method of social control is a new emergence in the process of evolution, and mental illness is the price we have to pay for being men and having the power of choice and the capacity for growth.

I believe that certain forms of mental illness, particularly those characterized by anxiety and conviction of sin, are not evils. They are instead manifestations of the power that makes for health. They are analogous to fever or inflammation in the body. I am thus very sure that the experience which plunged me into this new field of labor was mental illness of the most profound and unmistakable variety. I am equally sure that it was for me a problem-solving religious experience. My efforts to follow the leads derived from my own experience and check them against the experience of others has convinced me that my experience was by no means unique.

I believe that the real evil in functional mental illness is not to be found in discontent with one's imperfections, even when that discontent is carried to the point of severe disturbance, but in the sense of estrangement and isolation due to the presence of instinctual claims which can neither be controlled nor acknowledged for fear of condemnation. The aim of psychotherapy is not to get rid of the conflict by lowering the conscience threshold but to remove the sense of alienation by restoring the sufferer to the internalized fellowship of the best and thus setting him free to strive for his true objectives in life.

I believe that the paramount human need is that for love and that there is a law within which forbids us to be satisfied with any fellowship save that of the best. Religious experience is the sense of fellowship raised to its highest level, and religion is thus an inevitable consequence of the social nature of man. This means that religion is not to be explained in terms of relationship to parents. It is rather the reverse which is true. The parents are important to the young child because to a degree which is never repeated in the course of his existence they represent that in the universe upon which he is dependent for love and for protection. From the religious standpoint the aim of education is to lead the growing individual to transfer his loyalty from the finite to the infinite and to recognize that his parents are merely representatives of a higher loyalty, to which he owes unconditioned allegiance. For the religious man this higher loyalty is represented by his idea of God, and that idea stands for something which is operative in the lives of all men whether they recognize it or not. Ethical norms do not stand or fall with a belief in God, but they do not exist in a vacuum. They rest upon and are functions of the living relationships symbolized by such a belief, and they are validated by their long-run consequences in the lives of those who hold them.

VI

OBSERVATIONS
AND REFLECTIONS

THIS RECORD has thus far sought to present a simple, factual account. It has told the story of my life with a minimum of reflection and interpretation. There must therefore be a number of questions in the mind of anyone who has read the narrative carefully. Some of these questions call for consideration.

THE BASIC CONFLICT

The first of these questions will probably have to do with the basis of the conflict, the sexual hypersensitivity which caused me so much agony in the adolescent period. I thought of myself as having a "diseased mind" and of being a "wretch in direst need." Did I not perhaps exaggerate the trouble and work myself up into a morbid condition over something which was not so bad after all? Was not the sense of guilt a "needless and harmful intruder," to use Dr. Fosdick's phrase?[1] Was not a "measure of intelligent common sense about a small prohibitory detail" all that was needed? I have often wanted to think so. Nevertheless, it remains true that until the decision to study forestry and until Alice Batchelder came into my life, I was fighting a losing battle on a crucially important front. I was a really sick person. I

[1] *On Being a Real Person* (New York: Harper & Brothers, 1943), p. 150.

needed something more thorough-going than intelligent common sense; and the anxiety, the distress of mind, even when carried to the point of psychosis, was, as I see it, nature's way of seeking to effect the needed changes.

The present-day tendency to seek the solution of a troublesome sex drive by lowering the conscience threshold and looking upon sex as a natural desire to be lightly satisfied is something which seems to me to be a serious mistake. Such a solution takes little account of the principle which Professor Hocking sets forth so finely, that sex love, insofar as it finds its true meaning, approaches identity with religion.[2] It seeks somewhat the same thing, viz., union with the idealized other-than-self, and the health and meaning of love depend upon the common devotion to a common divinity.

From the biological standpoint it is to be borne in mind that the sex drive has to do with the perpetuation and improvement of the race. Since it is for this that the individual exists, and since in man the sex drive is not controlled physiologically, as in the lower animals, but by means of the "mores," the conscience, it is hardly to be wondered at that its control gives rise to difficult problems. Their solution is surely not to be found in easy self-indulgence, at least for those who are concerned with the realization of the personal and social potentialities that ought to be. For my own part, as I look back over the past, I have no regret for the anxiety and distress of mind which I suffered in those early years, but only for my stupidity and failure to learn the elements of self-discipline.

But does not such a view impose a terrible burden upon the adolescent and upon those who are responsible for his upbring-

[2] *Human Nature and Its Re-making* (New Haven: Yale University Press, 1923), chap. 42.

ing? Probably so. But the solution, as I see it, is to be found in Paul's doctrine of the spirit as contrasted with the law. The important consideration is what one is in process of becoming, and any man, no matter what his frailties, is worthy of honor insofar as he is moving to become better and is doing the best he can with what he has to work with.

My own experience may serve to call attention to the futility of merely imparting information in that which concerns sex education. The books which gave me trouble in my adolescent period were for the most part good books; but they supplied more information than I was able to handle at the time. It should be very clear that sex education is not a matter of instruction, but of psychotherapy. It is dependent not so much upon what the teacher says to the boy as upon what the boy is able to say to the teacher.

THE PASSAGES OF SCRIPTURE

Another question which may be raised has to do with the opening of the Bible and looking for guidance in the words upon which my eye happened to fall (see pp. 53-55). In one of my interviews with Dr. Elwood Worcester at the time I was leaving Westboro, I made an apologetic reference to the fact that I had done that. He rebuked me sharply. This was not just superstition, he said. While he would never encourage anyone to employ such a device, it was in his judgment a well-established fact that communications were sometimes received in this way.

I would not for a minute defend this as a practice. At the same time, I still believe that something more than coincidence was here involved. Those passages of Scripture and the other messages bore with amazing directness upon the questions uppermost in my mind. I am very sure that if I had started out to look for pertinent suggestions, it would have been difficult to find any that applied more aptly than those which came apparently by chance. However that may be, these "messages" had value regardless of the way they came.

Dr. Worcester, it should be said, was a convinced believer in psychic phenomena and a leader in the field of psychic research. I have myself long held the view that the religious *Weltanschauung* presupposes the survival of the personality and the existence of an organized spiritual world superior to our own. What I have questioned is the attempt to communicate with various discarnate spirits. My visits to a number of séances have impressed me with the fact that their procedures and beliefs, and the atmosphere which pervades them, make for a disorganized universe. For this reason I have looked upon them as unwholesome, except for the trained investigator, and I have deliberately avoided them. It is in my judgment of the essence of Christianity that prayer is directed to God "in the name of Christ," thus making for a centralized universe.

I am profoundly convinced of the purposive nature of the searching experiences through which I have passed. I am equally convinced that there is involved something more than blind striving, or *élan vitale*. For these beliefs my own experience furnishes evidence to me. I can hardly expect it to do so for others.

THE ACUTE EPISODES

A review of this record will show that I have passed through five psychotic episodes during which my thinking has been irrational in the extreme and my condition was such as to warrant the classification of "schizophrenic reaction, catatonic type." By that is meant that in sharp contrast to those forms of schizophrenia in which some adaptation to defeat and failure has been made and accepted, they were periods of seething emotion which tended either to make or break, periods in the development of the personality in which fate hung in the balance and destiny was in large measure determined.[3] Of these five psychotic episodes I believe I can say that, severe though they were, they have for me been problem-solving experiences. They have left me not worse but better (see pp. 59, 79-95, 114-20, 169-70, 176-77).

In addition to these five psychotic episodes there have been five major decisions which have been marked by deviation from the normal (see pp. 45-47, 50, 55, 56, 74-75).

All ten of these abnormal experiences began under the precise conditions which, for me at least, have characterized creative mental activity. There was intense interest in an important problem. There was also marked narrowing of attention, and prayer carried to the point of absorption. Such conditions are fertile in new ideas, but the creativity is obtained at the expense of structured experience. Perspective may be lost and wide limits set for the validity of inner promptings.[4] There is likely to be a radical change in the concept of the self, marked frequently by the sense of mystical identification, which leads some psychiatrists to explain such experiences in terms of "weak ego structure."

The beginning of the abnormal experience, regardless of its severity, and its most distinguishing characteristic, is to be found in what Professor Coe has called the "automatism." By this he meant the idea, or thought structure, which after a period of incubation in the region of dim awareness, leaps suddenly into

---

[3] A. T. Boisen, *Exploration of the Inner World* (New York: Harper & Brothers, 1952), chap. i; *Religion in Crisis and Custom* (New York: Harper & Brothers, 1955), chap. iv.

[4] Henri Delacroix, *op. cit.*, pp. 376 ff.

consciousness.[5] Such an idea may be interpreted as coming from a superhuman source, carrying authority because of its supposed origin. We have then the phenomena of "voices" so familiar to those who work in mental hospitals. So it was with me. The ideas which knocked me out so completely on October 6, 1920, came surging in as from an outside source and were so utterly different from anything I had read or heard before, that I accepted them as what George Fox called an "opening," or what Frank Buchman would call a "guidance." I was at first not uncritical, but I soon abandoned critical judgment and accepted as valid whatever came into my mind.

This abdication of reason before the authority of the automatism is, then, distinctive of the abnormal condition, especially in its acute forms. A better way to express it might be to say that critical judgment, though never absent, ascribes undue validity to the automatism, or insight, and feeling displaces reason and common sense. The unseen world of fantasy and feeling becomes the supposedly real world.

The automatism, as a psychological process, is found not only in the experience of schizophrenics. It is to be found also in the creative activities of poets and inventors and scientists. It is the mechanism involved in spiritistic phenomena.

It follows, therefore, that in the automatisms which characterize acute schizophrenic episodes, in those which may accompany the making of important decisions, and in those of poets, inventors, scientists, and religious leaders, we have a continuum

[5] George A. Coe, *Psychology of Religion* (Chicago: University of Chicago Press, 1916), p. 103; chap. xvi.

Eliot Dole Hutchinson, "The Phenomena of Insight in Relation to Religion," *Psychiatry*, VI: 4 (Nov. 1943), 347-57.

A. T. Boisen, *Exploration of the Inner World*, chaps. i and ii; *Religion in Crisis and Custom*, chaps. iv, v, and vii; "Onset in Acute Schizophrenia," *Psychiatry*, X: 2 (May 1947), 159-66.

of psychic events which differ from each other only in intensity, subject matter, and value.

SENSE IN THE NONSENSE

Dr. Adolph Meyer has said that he could listen with as much respect to the ideas of an excited schizophrenic as he could to those of an Oriental philosopher, because he knew that those ideas had meaning, and his job as a psychiatrist was to discover the sense in the nonsense.

As I look back upon the strange ideas which came flooding into my mind during the disturbed periods, I keep that principle in mind. But what an array of ideas and how bizarre and utterly meaningless some of them seem!

In any attempt at interpretation it should be noted that some of these ideas are characteristic of acute schizophrenia generally. Ideas of self-sacrifice, of death, of world disaster, of mystical identification, of rebirth, of reincarnation, of prophetic mission are to be found not only in my case but in other acutely disturbed schizophrenics also. As I have shown elsewhere,[6] such ideas seem to form a sort of constellation which is distinctive of acute schizophrenia. Where we find one of these ideas we are likely to find the others also. Such ideas do have meaning. Their basis may be found in the structure of the human psyche and in the constructive aspects of the schizophrenic experience. The idea of self-sacrifice and death, which is most frequent in schizophrenic thinking, represents quite accurately the loss or renunciation of something of supreme value, with which schizophrenic dis-

[6] *Exploration of the Inner World,* chap. i; "The Form and Content of Schizophrenic Thinking," *Psychiatry,* V: 1 (February 1942), 23-33; "Onset in Acute Schizophrenia," *Psychiatry,* X: 2 (May, 1947), 159-66; "Mystical Identification in Mental Disorder," *Psychiatry,* XV: 3 (August, 1952), 287-96.

turbances commonly begin. The idea of world disaster is the magnification of the personal death experience until it assumes cosmic proportions. The idea of rebirth stands for the inner meaning of acute schizophrenia, that of attempted renewal, or reorganization. The prophetic urge represents the world-wide outreach of vital religion, while cosmic identification comes with the sudden opening of the eyes to a staggering new insight, that even the most commonplace person is a social being, important beyond his wildest dreams.

These ideas symbolize the meaning of the acute schizophrenic experience in its typical, or generic manifestations, and the predominance of such ideas, when free from malignant tendencies such as suspicion, hostility, faultfinding, self-deception, wishful thinking, and eroticism, means usually that the healing forces are in operation, that hidden things are being brought to light, and that the sufferer is striving desperately to face what for him is ultimate Reality.

Thus interpreted, an acute schizophrenic episode assumes the character of religious experience. It becomes an attempt at thoroughgoing reorganization, beginning at the very center of one's being, an attempt which tends either to make or break the personality.

In addition to these generic ideas there were some which were peculiar to my own case, ideas which I have not encountered elsewhere either in my reading or in other cases with which I have dealt. Among these are the "theory of types" (see p. 105), that of "life in two cycles" (see p. 106), the idea of "levels of existence" (see p. 93), and the "family-of-four" (see p. 82). In most of these I see no special meaning. I am inclined to regard them as due to the play of fantasy when the mind is stirred by strong emotion at its deeper levels.

One of these ideas, however, has puzzled me not a little. I refer to that of the family-of-four. This idea sprang full-fledged into my mind just at the time when I seemed about to attain that for which I had been striving over seventeen long years. It called for a renunciation of that hope, and it recurred insistently in each one of the subsequent psychotic episodes. It really seemed as though some deeper self were trying to impart some urgent message. But when I sought to interpret it in accordance with longings of my own, there arose a conflict which eventuated in the psychosis of 1930.

What specific meaning this idea had in the later episodes is by no means clear, but for the earlier disturbance of 1920, the situation in which I found myself offers a clue. It is to be borne in mind that Alice was a professional religious worker, a representative of the organization which, at the time I first knew her, was in charge of about all the personal counseling which was being done in our colleges. It is also to be recognized that I was a really sick person who had come to her for help. This help she at first refused but eventually granted. She tried, however, to keep the relationship on a professional basis. She wrote to me on her official stationery, and she corrected me sharply whenever I assumed that anything beyond a professional relationship was involved. But that assumption was there in her mind, too, I think. She assumed that she would have to marry me to give the needed help. But for her, marriage was to be thought of only under certain conditions. I must first prove my manhood and the devotion I professed. This I failed to do. As a woman of integrity and courage she took that as her answer. At the same time, there was an obligation which she recognized. I had entered the ministry under conditions in which she was involved. She therefore felt a certain responsibility for me.

But from the beginning I had told her that it was her help I needed and that I would never accept anything from her that she could not give freely. I had even gone so far, during a brief psychotic episode, as to try to give her to another man.

The idea of the family-of-four might then represent the feeling deep down within me that there ought to be a way for her, or for her prototype, to give the needed help without having to sacrifice herself in a loveless marriage. And there ought to be a way for me, or for my prototype, to receive such help without having to undergo the frustration which I had suffered.

What was involved in this idea of the family-of-four would then be somewhat like the Freudian concept of the "transference" relationship, which had struck me so forcibly when I first heard of it during my hospitalization at Westboro (see p. 104). Freud had found that in cases of neurotic illness in which treatment is effective, it is to be expected that the patient may become attached to the physician and that this attachment may even go so far as to become love. If this happens, it is not to be regarded as a cause for embarrassment, but rather as a source of healing which is to be accepted and utilized as part of the process of treatment. It must then be resolved before the cure is complete. There are difficulties in this interpretation, but of one thing at least I am sure. My love for Alice Batchelder has been for me a source of healing.

The family-of-four was of course a crazy idea and there may or may not be sense in the nonsense, but in it and in the experience out of which it sprang I see one principle which is eternally true. I am thinking of the Freudian teaching that the transference relationship must be satisfactorily resolved before the cure is complete. I am thinking of the old Dante-Beatrice story, in which the poet had to pass through the fire before he could enter Paradise and join the woman he worshiped. I am thinking of Professor Hocking's insistence that love between man and woman can be truly happy only when each is a free and autonomous being, dependent not upon the other but upon God. Where, on the other hand, a man's love for a woman is such that he draws not from the common source of strength, but clings to her, that man is not worthy of her. That principle is sound, and it may help in the interpretation of the experience of 1920. It was necessary for me to pass through the purgatorial fires of a horrifying psychosis before I could set foot in my promised land of creative activity.

EPILOGUE
THE GUIDING HAND

FIFTY-EIGHT YEARS have now passed since I first met Alice Batchelder. During all these years the thought of her has been central with me. Through her I was led into the Christian ministry, and with the passing of the years my love for her has become more and more interwoven with my religious faith. To her my thoughts turn, as I now bring this book to a close.

The writing of this record has been no easy matter. Sometimes it has been for me like a day of judgment. It is distressingly clear that there has been on my part a succession of blunders and failures. The memory of Ponemah and the ill-starred expedition after arbutus brings with it especial pain. And yet I have no regret. Our evil has been overcome for good. If it had not been for my failure on that occasion, Alice and I might have been married, and with her help I might have become a passably successful minister. But so far as I am concerned, there would have been no new light upon the interrelatedness of mental disorder and religious experience. Neither would there have been for me any clinical-training movement.

I am reminded of the ancient Joseph story, in which Joseph breaks down and weeps at the sight of the brothers who had sold him into slavery. He wept, it is clear, because he had caught a glimpse of the Love beyond that of father and mother, which even through apparent disaster had been shaping his destiny for good. He was thus able to say to his brothers, "Be not angry with yourselves because ye sold me hither. So now, it was not you that sent me hither, but God."

I would surely be a man of little faith if I did not recognize in this story the guiding hand of an Intelligence beyond our own.

For whatever of value may have been accomplished, Alice should share fully in the credit. We were, I think, as actors in some great drama whose roles are interdependent. In all that I have done she has been an indispensable factor, and hers the harder and more difficult role. She had to suffer for my mistakes and slowness of mind. She was a rarely gifted woman who, on my account, never found her highest usefulness. So, at least, I interpret this story. For me, on the other hand, there has been movement, variety, the challenge of interesting tasks, and some measure of recognition.

My mind goes back to the dedication of my *Exploration of the Inner World,* which was written during the searchings of heart which I underwent at the time of Alice's death. I recognize that I was suffering at the time from a deep sense of personal failure and that my normal judgment was impaired. Nevertheless, I consider that dedication to be a true expression of my deepest feeling and best insight. It was indeed for her sake that I undertook my venture into the unexplored. Her compassion on me, her wisdom, her courage, and her unswerving fidelity have made possible the measure of success achieved. And my love for her has been linked with all that is best and holiest in this life of mine. One thing only would I change. Instead of just the initials, I would write in her full name, as I have done in this book, that all may know of the love and honor in which I shall ever hold her.

WRITINGS OF ANTON T. BOISEN

1910

"The Commercial Hickories" (Bulletin 80, *U.S. Forest Service*), Washington, D.C., Government Printing Office, 64 pp. Written with J. A. Newlin.

1912

"A Rural Survey in Missouri," New York: Presbyterian Board of Home Missions, 42 pp. Written with Fred Eastman.

"A Rural Survey in Tennessee," New York: Presbyterian Board of Home Missions, 48 pp.

1916

"Factors in the Decline of the Country Church," *American Journal of Sociology*, Vol. 22, No. 2, 177-92.

1923

"What a Country Minister Ought to Know," *Christian Work*, Vol. 114, No. 25, June 23.

"Religious Experience and Mental Disorder," *Mental Hygiene*, Vol. 7, No. 2, April, 307-11.

1924

Book Review of Norman Thomas's *The Conscientious Objector*, in *Adult Bible Class Magazine*, September.

"The Church and the Sick Soul," *Adult Bible Class Magazine*, May.

1925

"In Defense of Mr. Bryan: A Personal Confession by a Liberal Clergyman," *American Review*, May.

"Escaping from the Blues," *Adult Bible Class Magazine*, May.

1926

"A Challenge to Our Seminaries," *Christian Work*, Vol. 120, No. 4, January 23.

LIFT UP YOUR HEARTS: A Service-book for Use in Hospitals, Boston: Pilgrim Press, 96 pp.

"Personality Changes and Upheavals Arising Out of the Sense of Personal Failure," *American Journal of Psychiatry*, Vol. 5, No. 4, April, 331-51.

1927

"Evangelism in the Light of Psychiatry," *Journal of Religion*, Vol. 7, No. 1, January, 76-80.

"Exploration of the Inner World," *Chicago Theological Seminary Register*, January.

"Clinical Training for Theological Students," *C. T. S. Register*, November.

1928

"The Psychiatric Approach to the Study of Religion," *Religious Education*, March.

"The Study of Mental Disorders As the Basis for a Program of Moral and Religious Education," *Religious Education*, April.

"The Sense of Isolation in Mental Disorder: Its Religious Significance," *American Journal of Sociology*, Vol. 33, No. 4, January, 555-67.

1929

"The Woman to Whom Jesus First Appeared," *C. T. S. Register*, March.

1930

"Theological Education via the Clinic," *Religious Education*, March.

"Religious Work in a State Hospital," *Bulletin of the Massachusetts Department of Mental Diseases*, April.

1932

"The Church and Sick Souls," *C. T. S. Register*, January.

HYMNS OF HOPE AND COURAGE, A Revised and Enlarged Edition of *Lift Up Your Hearts*, Boston: Pilgrim Press, 112 pp.

"Prayer," *C. T. S. Register*, March.

"The Problem of Values in the Light of Psychopathology," *American Journal of Sociology*, Vol. 38, No. 1, July, 251-68.

"Schizophrenia and Religious Experience," Elgin State Hospital: *Collected and Contributed Papers*, Vol. I, 70-83.

"What Happened on the Road to Damascus," *Adult Bible Class Magazine*, October.

1933

"Experiential Aspects of Dementia Praecox," *American Journal of Psychiatry*, Vol. 13, No. 3, November, 542-78.

1934

Book review of Richard Cabot's *The Meaning of Right and Wrong*, in *C. T. S. Register*, January.

"Christian Perfectionism," *C. T. S. Register*, January.

1935

"The New Evangelism," *C. T. S. Register*, March.

1936

EXPLORATION OF THE INNER WORLD, Chicago: Willett, Clark & Co., xi + 321 pp.; New York: Harper & Brothers, 1952.

1937

"God and the Cross in Human Experience," *C. T. S. Register*, March.

1938

"Types of Dementia Praecox: A Study in Psychiatric Classification," *Psychiatry*, Vol. 1, No. 2, May, 233-36.

1939

"The Holy Rollers Come to Town," *C. T. S. Register*, January.

"Conversion and Mental Health," *International Journal of Religious Education*, January.

"Religion and Hard Times," *Social Action*, March.

"Economic Distress and Religious Experience," *Psychiatry*, Vol. 2, No. 2, May, 185-94.

Book review of James S. Plant's *Personality and the Culture Pattern*, in *Psychiatry*, Vol. 2, No. 2, May, 294-96.

1940

"Religious Education and Human Nature," *Religious Education*, January-March.

"The Psychiatrist Challenges the Minister," *C. T. S. Register*, January.

"Divided Protestantism in a Midwest County: A Study in the Natural History of Religion," *Journal of Religion*, Vol. 20, No. 4, October, 360-81.

1941

"Theology in the Light of Psychiatric Experience," *Crozer Quarterly*, Vol. 18, No. 1, 47-61.

Book review of C. G. Jung's *Integration of the Personality*, in *Review of Religion*.

1942

"Form and Content of Schizophrenic Thinking," *Psychiatry*, Vol. 5, No. 1, February, 23-33.

"Religion and Personality Adjustments," *Psychiatry*, Vol. 5, No. 2, May, 209-18.

"Personality Adjustments in a Country Parish," *C. T. S. Register*, January.

"Sin and Salvation in the Light of Psychiatric Experience," *Journal of Religion*, Vol. 22, No. 3, July, 288-301.

Book review of Erich Fromm's *Escape from Freedom*, in *Psychiatry*, Vol. 5, No. 1, February, 113-17.

Book review of William Lowe Bryan's *Wars of Families of Minds*, in *C. T. S. Register*, January.

1944

"George Fox among the Doctors," *Friends Intelligencer*, Vol. 101, No. 23.

"Niebuhr and Fosdick on Sin," *C. T. S. Register*, March.

"Conscientious Objectors: Their Morale in Church-operated Service Units," *Psychiatry*, Vol. 7, No. 3, August, 215-24.

1945

"Clinical Training for Theological Students," *C. T. S. Register*, January.

"What War Does to Religion," *Religion in Life*, Summer issue.

"Can a Sick World Get Well?" *Christian Century*, July 11.

"Co-operative Inquiry in Religion," *Religious Education,* October. Reissued in *Journal of Pastoral Care,* Spring, 1951.

Book review of Wilhelm Reich's *Character Analysis,* and *The Sexual Revolution,* in *Psychiatry,* Vol. 8, No. 4.

1946

PROBLEMS IN RELIGION AND LIFE, New York and Nashville: Abingdon-Cokesbury Press, 159 pp.

Religion and Mental Health: A Beginning Course—mimeographed for private circulation, Elgin State Hospital, 150 pp.

Religion and Mental Health: Collected Papers—mimeographed for private circulation, Elgin State Hospital, 150 pp.

1947

"Self-Expression," *The Pastor* (Nashville, Tenn.), April.

Book review of Charles Morris's *Signs, Language and Behavior,* in *Psychiatry,* Vol. 10, No. 2, 228-30.

Book review of Roy G. Hoskins's *Biology of Schizophrenia,* in *Journal of Religion,* Vol. 27, No. 4, October, 298-99.

1948

"The Service of Worship in a Mental Hospital: Its Therapeutic Significance," *Journal of Clinical Pastoral Work,* Vol. 2, No. 1.

"The Minister As Counselor," *Journal of Pastoral Care,* Vol. 2, No. 1.

1950

HYMNS OF HOPE AND COURAGE, Fourth Revised and Enlarged Edition, Chicago Theological Seminary, Chicago 37, Ill., 128 pp.

1951

"Anxiety: Its Therapeutic Significance," *Journal of Pastoral Care,* Vol. 5, No. 2, Summer issue.

"The Challenge to Our Seminaries," reprinted from *Christian Work,* January 23, 1926, in *Journal of Pastoral Care,* Vol. 5, No. 1, Spring issue.

"Co-operative Inquiry in Religion," reprinted from *Religious Education,* October, 1945, in *Journal of Pastoral Care,* Spring issue.

"Development and Validation of Religious Faith," *Psychiatry,* Vol 14, No. 4, November, 455-62.

"Religion and the Unconscious in Freud, Jung and Fromm," *Pastoral Psychology*, September.

1952

"What Did Jesus Think of Himself?" *Journal of Bible and Religion*, Vol. 20, No. 1, January, 7-12.

"Mystical Identification in Mental Disorder," *Psychiatry*, Vol. 15, No. 3, 287-96.

"George Albert Coe," *Pastoral Psychology*, October.

1953

"William James' Psychology of Religion: Its Present Status," *Pastoral Care*, Vol. 7, No. 3, Fall issue.

"Religious Symptomatology in a Schizophrenic Breakdown," comments on article by Robert Leslie, *Pastoral Psychology*, Vol. 4, No. 37, October.

1954

"Group Therapy: Elgin Plan," *Pastoral Psychology*, March.

"Schizophrenic Ideation As Striving toward a Solution of Conflict," *Journal of Clinical Psychology*, Vol. 10, No. 4, October, 289-91. Written with R. L. Jenkins and Maurice Lorr.

1955

RELIGION IN CRISIS AND CUSTOM: A Sociological and Psychological Study, New York: Harper & Brothers, xv + 271 pp.

"Psychiatric Screening of Theological Students," comments on article by Carl Christensen, *Pastoral Care*, Fall issue.

1956

"Pathological Anxiety," comments on article by Paul Tillich, *Pastoral Psychology*, March.

1958

"Religious Experience and Psychological Conflict," *American Psychologist*, Vol. 13, No. 10, October, 368-70.

1960

"Therapeutic Value of Hymns," *Pastoral Psychology*, March.